The
Parent
Lifesaver

# The Parent Lifesaver

## Practical HELP for Everyday Childhood Problems

## Dr. Todd Cartmell

Baker Books

A Division of Baker Book House Co
Grand Rapids, Michigan 49516

Published by Baker Books
a division of Baker Book House Company
P.O. Box 6287, Grand Rapids, MI 49516-6287

Printed in the United States of America

**Library of Congress Cataloging-in-Publication Data**

Cartmell, Todd, 1962–
    The parent lifesaver / Todd Cartmell.
        p.    cm.
    Includes bibliographical references.
    ISBN 0-8010-5826-0 (pbk.)
    1. Child rearing. 2. Discipline of children. 3. Child rearing—Religious
aspects—Christianity. 4. Discipline of children—Religious aspects—Christianity. 5. Problem children—Behavior modification. I. Title
HQ769.C34145   1998                            98-24536

This book is not intended as a substitution for professional evaluation and treatment.
If your child is experiencing significant behavioral or emotional problems, please consult a mental health professional.

Scripture is from the HOLY BIBLE, NEW INTERNATIONAL VERSION®. NIV®.
Copyright © 1973, 1978, 1984 by International Bible Society. Used by permission of
Zondervan Publishing House. All rights reserved.

For current information about all releases from Baker Book House, visit our web site:
http://www.bakerbooks.com

# Contents

# Preface

Parenting is one of the most wonderful experiences you can imagine. It brings more joy, meaning, and fulfillment to life than you could possibly have anticipated. Yet it also prompts feelings of frustration, concern, and sometimes inadequacy. There's no way around it. Being a good parent is hard work. Yet it's worth every ounce of effort and it's something most of us want desperately to be. And I believe that we can.

As a psychologist I have had the privilege of working with many families and have observed not only the joys but also the hurt, frustration, and disappointment accompanying life's adventures and challenges. Some families encounter more challenges than others, but all of us need a little help now and then. I've designed this book to be a "lifesaver" for you when you need that help. Used properly, a lifesaver not only brings you back to the surface of the water once you have gone under, but it also keeps you from going under in the first place. In this way, the principles and tools discussed in this book are designed to help you both *prevent* problems from developing and *respond* quickly and effectively when they do arise.

This book incorporates many helpful ideas gleaned from research with children during the past two decades and is intended for use with children between the ages of three and twelve. Designed to be as practical as possible, it allows you to put these valuable tools to work with your children right away. As you develop your understanding of the factors that influence child behavior and the importance of applying biblical principles to your parenting efforts, you'll find many helpful ideas for how to effectively respond to even the type of childhood behavior that increases your daily GHGR (that's your grey hair growth rate!).

It is my desire that this book will serve as a valuable resource to you as you guide your children and your family through the challenges of life in a biblical, thoughtful, and effective manner.

# Acknowledgments

I am most grateful to my parents who have provided me with a wonderful Christian model of what parenting is all about. Many thanks to my friend and colleague Steven Vincent, Psy.D., for proofreading this manuscript and offering his many helpful suggestions. Thanks also to my many colleagues and supervisors over the years who have helped to shape my thinking and approach to working with children, parents, and families. Most of all, I would like to express my love and appreciation to my wife, Lora, and to our two children, Jacob and Luke, for their support and encouragement in allowing me the time to complete this project.

# You Need a Plan

## *How to Get Started in the Right Direction*

By wisdom a house is built,
  and through understanding it is established.
                                         Proverbs 24:3

ey, you kids! Come back here right now!" Mrs. Anderson shouted down the grocery store aisle at her five-year-old daughter, Julie, and her friend Laura, who had decided to explore the grocery store without parental supervision. Julie had pulled this kind of thing on Mrs. Anderson before. "With a friend here," Mrs. Anderson had reasoned, "surely she won't do it this time." In a hurry and with a toddler in the cart on the verge of crying, Mrs. Anderson found herself in hot pursuit of her two runaways and about one step short of exploding into tears. *She didn't have a plan.*

Mrs. Hudson knew that eight-year-old Sammy had a problem staying put when accompanying her to the grocery store. To solve this problem, Mrs. Hudson devised a

simple set of grocery store rules. She explained them to
Sammy one evening at home and they rehearsed them,
pretending their house was the grocery store. Mrs. Hudson
also asked Sammy to help her make a list of possible negative consequences for breaking the rules and rewards for
following them. They decided that Sammy could have his
favorite dessert after dinner the first two times he followed
the grocery store rules. Mrs. Hudson told Sammy that once
he learned how to follow the rules, he could have a friend
come with him to the grocery store and come over to play
afterward. With a system of rewards and consequences in
place, Mrs. Hudson took Sammy to the grocery store for a
"practice trip" and showed him how to get things off the
shelves for her and place them gently in the cart. Sammy
loved it. *Mrs. Hudson had a plan.*

Eleven-year-old Randy's room was a disaster. In some
places, things were piled up a foot deep and strange odors
were starting to seep out from under the door. Mrs. Burgess
had talked to Randy about his room in the past but their
discussions produced little action. "I'm going to talk with
your father about this," she said to Randy in an angry voice,
not knowing what else to say. Randy just looked at his
mother with mild amusement, unaffected by her attempts
to prod him into action. When Mrs. Burgess discussed the
issue with her husband, he didn't see Randy's room as much
of a problem. "I was the same way when I was his age. Boys
will be boys. Just shut the door," was his reply to his wife's
complaints. *As a couple, they didn't have a plan.*

Mr. and Mrs. Johnson sat down to discuss Mrs. Johnson's concern over their eleven-year-old son's room. Although the room didn't bother Mr. Johnson as much as it
did Mrs. Johnson, they decided that some bottom-line
rules for room tidiness would be appropriate. They decided
to make an appointment with their son, Scott, to discuss

the issue. After treating him to a hamburger and fries on the appointed night, they sat down and talked about what the rules for Scott's room should be, given the fact that he is almost a teenager. Mr. and Mrs. Johnson listened carefully to Scott's point of view and tried to understand his feelings about wanting his room to be his own private space. However, they also shared their concerns about cleanliness and about freshly washed clothes getting hopelessly wrinkled and dirty clothes not making it to the hamper. Together, they decided on several bottom-line "room rules" with which everyone could live. The rules showed respect for general principles of sanitation and placed the responsibility on Scott to get his clothes to the hamper when they needed to be washed. They all agreed that instead of Mrs. Johnson nagging Scott about his room, there would be a room inspection every Friday after dinner. If the room passed the inspection, then everything was fine. If the room failed the inspection, then Scott not only had to immediately correct the room violations, but he had to tidy up his brother's room as well. *Mr. and Mrs. Johnson had a plan.*

Thud! Ms. Simpson, a single mom, heard the unmistakable sound of a hard object hitting the wall. Her four-year-old son, Lonnie, had a bad habit of throwing his toys, and the living-room wall was covered with the scrapes and nicks to prove it. Lonnie had been playing quietly for about fifteen minutes before breaking the silence by launching one of his Matchbox cars into flight. Ms. Simpson exploded into the living room, frustrated by Lonnie's refusal to play appropriately with his toys. "You're getting a spanking this time, mister," she shouted. *She didn't have a plan.*

Ms. Gibson had noticed that Holly, her four-year-old daughter, was developing a habit of throwing her toys. She decided to designate two soft balls that could be thrown indoors without a problem. Anything else was not to be thrown indoors. She explained these new rules to Holly and gave her frequent "pop quizzes" about which toys could be thrown inside. When she saw Holly throw these balls, Ms. Gibson got in the habit of immediately going over to her and telling her that she had done a good job of deciding which toy to throw. When Holly threw an "off-limits" toy, Ms. Gibson decided that Holly would immediately serve a Time-Out and lose the privilege of playing with that toy for the remainder of the day. *Ms. Gibson had a plan.*

## Proactive versus Reactive

What is the difference between the parents who responded to these common childhood behaviors effectively and those who did not? They are all good parents. They all love their children. They are all doing their best to teach their children appropriate behaviors. The difference is that the parents who responded ineffectively have developed a *reactive* parenting style. Instead of thinking ahead and developing a plan for addressing a problem behavior, they simply react. All of us have done this at one time or another and for many of us, this is our predominant style of addressing problem behaviors. If it ain't broke, don't fix it. If it breaks, respond to it as well as possible at the time.

In contrast, the other parents have developed a *proactive* style of parenting. When a problem behavior first develops, they start by putting together a plan. Moms and dads discuss the issue together to make sure that they are both thinking about the problem in the same way. Proactive parents try to figure out what may be causing the problem. They also make sure that they, as parents, are modeling appropriate behavior. Then, when possible, they try to figure out ways to prevent the problem from recurring in the future. They also decide what they would like their child to *start* doing and teach him or her to do this behavior in a fun way. They make sure that the desired behaviors are regularly rewarded when they happen, even if this only means saying, "Thank you" or "Great job for listening the first time" when they see the behavior. They also decide on the most effective negative consequences that can be used to follow the inappropriate behavior and use them consistently. As you can see, this proactive style is a simple and strategic way to address problematic childhood behavior, and a proactive approach is usually an effective one.

*A proactive approach is usually an effective one.*

## You Need a Plan

My wife, Lora, and I were having dinner one evening with another couple from our church. As we were eating and talking about many things, the topic of child rearing came up. Our friends told us about a class they had taken on parenting and I asked them what the most helpful part of the class was for them. Their answer was insightful. They said that the class had given them a plan. Now they had something *to do* instead of just being told what *not to do*. They felt like they knew where they were going and had some idea of how to get there.

Why is it so important to have a plan? Because parenting can be tough. My pastor has compared parenting to one of those games where you hold a mallet and try to hit the little gophers as they pop up out of their holes. The goal is to hit as many as you can. The problem is that every time you hit one, another pops out, just out of reach. As soon as you hit that one, another one pops out, then another and another. Parenting is kind of the same thing. You solve a little problem here. Then another one develops over there. As soon as you've taken care of that one, there's something else. It never ends.

Having a plan, then, is an important thing. Author and speaker Lawrence Peter once said, "If you don't know where you are going, you will probably end up somewhere else." A plan gives you a target and spells out the steps you need to take to get there. Having a plan means approaching the joy and responsibility of parenting in a thoughtful and deliberate manner. It means preventing problems whenever possible instead of always reacting to them after things have exploded. It means actively teaching children appropriate behavior rather than only reactively punishing them for inappropriate behavior. It means relating to and communicating with your children in a healthy way and providing them with a daily model of appropriate adult behavior. Having a plan means being proactive instead of reactive. And developing a plan is what this book is all about.

## Start with the End in Mind

As best-selling author Stephen Covey has pointed out, it is very helpful to start with the end in mind.[1] This is true, for example, when you play a game of chess or paint a picture. The end, of course, is to win your game of chess or to paint a beautiful picture. The primary difference between these two activities is the amount of control you have over the outcome. Painting involves you, your paint, and the canvas; the only obstacles to a perfect painting lie within yourself and your own skill level. In a game of chess, it is a different situation. You are playing with another person, and while you control your own moves, you do not control your opponent's moves.

Parenting is like chess in this way. While you have control of and responsibility for your own behaviors, there are several factors over which you *do not* have control. Genetic inheritance, environmental influences, and your child's free will offer three examples of factors that you cannot completely control. Like it or not, you cannot guarantee the type of person that your child will ultimately choose to be. As a father this thought sometimes scares me, but more importantly, it wakes me up to realize the importance of my influence on my children *right now!* I cannot control all of the factors that will influence them, nor can I prevent them from making a bad decision or two. Therefore, if the end that I have in mind is to guarantee "perfect" children who will grow up to be "perfect" adults, I am setting myself up for disappointment.

I suggest you strive for a different end. Because you cannot control your child's ultimate destiny, it is even more important that you are wise and diligent with what you can control. And you can control a lot. You have complete control over the type of parent that you will be! For example, you can repeat the mistakes your parents made with you. Or you can choose to stop old, unproductive patterns and replace them with new, healthy ways of relating with your children. You can allow yourself to be caught up in your work and other obligations, thereby forfeiting priceless time with your children. Or you can choose to maintain an appropriate balance between time spent at work and time spent with your family. When your kids are grown, you can look back on your parenting years with regret, wishing that you could do it over again. Or you can look back fondly, satisfied that you were the best parent that you could be.

Having a realistic end in mind is crucial. If you try to achieve too much or try to achieve the impossible, failure is inevitable. Your overall plan as a parent should not be to have perfect children. Neither should your plan be for you to be a perfect parent. None of us can ever reach those goals.

Your plan should be for you to be the best parent that you can be.

> You have complete control over the type of parent that you will be.

You can achieve that! Being the best parent you can be does not require perfection. It requires honesty, humility, perseverance, forgiveness, and trust that God will bless your best efforts. It means being willing to learn new ways of handling difficult situations. It means listening to your children and to your spouse. It means replacing ineffective methods of communication and discipline with more effective approaches. It means forgiving yourself when you make a mistake, brushing yourself off, and trying again. Henry Ford, the legendary car manufacturer, wisely observed, "Failure is the opportunity to begin again, more intelligently." More importantly, the Bible tells us the following about God's ability to work in us and strengthen us:

[He] is able to do immeasurably more than all we ask or imagine, according to his power that is at work within us.

Ephesians 3:20

He who began a good work in you will carry it on to completion until the day of Christ Jesus.

Philippians 1:6

I can do everything through him who gives me strength.

Philippians 4:13

God has great plans for you as a parent! If you follow biblical principles, adopt a realistic and optimistic attitude, turn mistakes into lessons, and are not allergic to hard work, you *can* become the best parent that you can be! And this will help your child become the best person that he or she can be.

## Five Key Ingredients

So, how do you become the best parent that you can be? Picture a baseball diamond. There are four bases centered around a pitcher's mound (see figure 1). This is a perfect picture to help you remember five key ingredients that will help you become the best parent you can be.

Figure 1

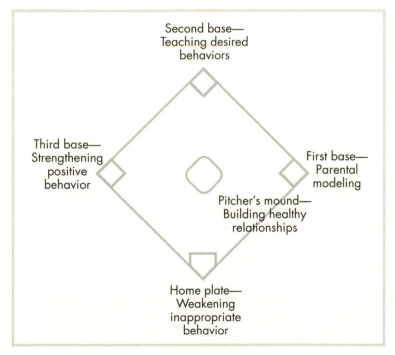

Second base—
Teaching desired
behaviors

Third base—
Strengthening
positive
behavior

First base—
Parental
modeling

Pitcher's mound—
Building healthy
relationships

Home plate—
Weakening
inappropriate
behavior

Just as a baseball game begins with the first pitch, so we must begin with the ingredient symbolized by the pitcher's mound: *building healthy relationships*. You can't have a base-ball game without a pitcher, and you won't have effective biblical parenting without first building a healthy relation-ship with your child. This involves striving for a *quality* re-lationship as well as spending a reasonable *quantity* of time with your child. That's right, both quality and quantity are important. It is hard to build a relationship with somebody that you never see, or with somebody that you see but sel-dom relate to. While some life circumstances (e.g., divorce) can legitimately make it difficult to spend a great deal of time with your child, it is important that you do the very best that you can to make that relationship a priority. Kids have a funny way of sens-ing whether or not they are important to you.

If we are to be godly leaders in our family, we must lead by example. There is no other way.

Once you have hit the first pitch of relationship building, your next stop is first base. Here you must take a look at the behavior you *model* for your children. Like what? Your relationship with God. Your relationship with your spouse. Your style of communicating with family members. The priority you place on spiritual disciplines (e.g., prayer, Bible study, etc.). The way that you express yourself when you are angry. Your method for solving problems. Your bad habits. Your "col-orful" language. Your choice of television shows. Your pri-orities. The list goes on and on. When we take a close look at our own behavior, the mystery may not be why our children are acting as badly as they do, it may be why their behavior is not worse! A parent's behavior affects a child's behavior. If we are to be godly leaders in our family, we must lead by example. There is no other way.

As we round second base, we now consider whether we are *teaching* our children how to behave appropriately. This may sound simple, but it is a very helpful idea. It is far easier for my four-year-old son to learn to play a game that he has never seen before if I show him the game pieces, explain the rules, demonstrate the movement around the board, and even go through a few practice rolls of the die than if I just throw him the box and expect him to know how to play. If this is true for a game, then it is even more true for more complicated life situations such as controlling a temper, curtailing impulses to throw a toy, or curbing the temptation to tell a lie. Children have many things to learn and life never ceases to provide challenging learning situations. If I take the time to teach my son how to play a game of Monopoly, then perhaps I should consider spending some concentrated time teaching him how to exhibit behaviors that are far more important and far more difficult. If I have not done this, then I should not be surprised that I do not see these desired behaviors happening more often.

Third base is just as important. As we will soon see, behaviors that are *reinforced,* or *strengthened,* tend to happen more frequently than behaviors that are not. Just as plants are designed to bloom when they are watered, appropriate behaviors will happen more often when they are consistently noticed and reinforced. This step is often overlooked in attempts to address childhood misbehavior. Many parents rely on discipline designed to stomp out inappropriate behavior when a far more effective approach would aim to *increase* desired behavior. If your plant is withering, check your water jug.

Finally, once we reach home plate, we need to take a look at how we can most effectively use negative consequences to *weaken inappropriate behaviors*. Punishment may be given in a way that actually reinforces rather than deters negative behavior, and sometimes negative consequences are simply ineffective or loaded with negative side effects. Other times, inappropriate behavior may be accidentally rewarded. So, just as it is important to be actively reinforcing desired behaviors, it is equally important to be responding to negative behaviors in a thoughtful and effective manner.

These are five key ingredients that must be a part of your plan if you want to achieve your goal of being the best parent you can be. Difficulties in any of these areas contribute not only to childhood misbehavior, but to a variety of other problems as well. You must start by making sure that you are relating to your children in a healthy way and modeling a genuine Christian lifestyle. Then, you do your best to teach your children the behaviors they need to learn, consistently rewarding them for doing those behaviors, and providing effective negative consequences for inappropriate behaviors. Remember the baseball diamond and you've got your plan.

## Put It in Writing

Earlier you couldn't hit a target you didn't have. But now that you have established your goal you must figure out how you will get there. This book is full of ideas that will help you achieve your goal of being the best parent that you can be. But it always helps to put your plan in writing. The Parenting Plan in appendix A is intended for just that. You can use your Parenting Plan in two ways: to evaluate your *overall* progress in becoming the best parent you can be and to evaluate your progress in addressing a *specific* problem behavior, such as temper tantrums or sibling conflicts. Different parents will need to improve in different areas and husbands and wives will probably find that they each have a different combination of strengths and weaknesses. Take the time now to complete sections A and B of your Parenting Plan, evaluating yourself either in an overall sense *or* in relation to the way you are handling a specific problem behavior. In section A, identify your goal as either to become the best parent you can be or to help improve *(fill in the problem behavior)*.

As you continue to move through this book, you will be able to complete section C. The following chapters are devoted to giving you the tools and specific ideas that you need to make positive changes in each of the five key parenting areas. As you read, identify specific tools and behaviors that will help you improve in the areas in which you need improvement and fill in the corresponding blanks in section C. By the time you are finished, your plan should be complete and you will be well on your way to achieving your parenting goals.

For example, take a look at the Sample Parenting Plan on page 25. As you can see, Steve felt that he needed improvement in every area in his effort to help his son learn to express angry feelings more appropriately (i.e., a specific problem behavior). He then wrote down two *specific* steps that he could take to make the needed changes in each area. Among other things, Steve planned to:

1. Take Johnny out to breakfast or lunch once a month.
2. Learn to express his own angry feelings more appropriately.
3. Teach Johnny simple steps for expressing angry feelings.
4. Use verbal rewards when Johnny uses his new steps.
5. Use Time-Out consistently when Johnny expresses his anger in inappropriate ways.

Steve had developed a plan. Rather than shouting at Johnny or haphazardly grounding or spanking him when he throws a tantrum, Steve is now taking a far more balanced and effective approach. In addition, Steve is taking purposeful steps toward improving his relationship with his son and will be modeling healthy biblical behavior. Can you imagine what it will be like when Steve and his wife, Cindy, develop a plan together?

*A plan is only useful if you stick to it.*

I must mention one more thing. A plan is only useful if you stick to it. If you are married, I suggest that you and your spouse develop your plans together and then agree to help and encourage each other in the specific areas where you each need to improve. Agree to hold each other accountable and give each other permission to point out times when you did a great job *and* times when you could have done better. If you are a single parent, then share your Parenting Plan with a close friend or family member and ask that person to check with you periodically as to how you are doing in meeting your goal.

Take your Parenting Plan seriously. We take our jobs seriously. Many of us take sports and hobbies seriously. Some of us even take television shows seriously. Someone once said that the most valuable things in life are not even things at all. There is no doubt that your relationship with your children is one of the most valuable things that you will ever possess. So as you read, put some serious thought and action into your Parenting Plan and become the best parent that you can be!

# Sample Parenting Plan

**Parent Name:** *Steve*

**A. Goal:** *To help improve the way Johnny expresses angry feelings*

**B. Areas to evaluate (check all that apply):**

| Area | Strong | Needs Improvement |
|---|---|---|
| 1. Building healthy relationships (e.g., quality, quantity, communication) | ☐ | ☒ |
| 2. Modeling biblical and appropriate behavior (e.g., marital relationship, anger-control, priorities, etc.) | ☐ | ☒ |
| 3. Teaching children appropriate behaviors | ☐ | ☒ |
| 4. Effectively strengthening appropriate behaviors | ☐ | ☒ |
| 5. Effectively weakening inappropriate behaviors | ☐ | ☒ |

**C. Ways to improve in each area:**

| Area | Ways to Improve |
|---|---|
| 1. Building healthy relationships | a. *Take Johnny out to breakfast the first Saturday of each month.* <br> b. *Build a model and shoot more baskets together.* |
| 2. Modeling biblical and appropriate behavior | a. *Improve my expression of angry feelings. Consult with pastor or therapist if needed.* <br> b. *Watch less television and interact with family more.* |
| 3. Teaching children appropriate behaviors | a. *Talk with Cindy (wife) and develop steps for appropriate anger-control.* <br> b. *Teach steps to Johnny and practice.* |
| 4. Effectively strengthening appropriate behaviors | a. *Use the Pour It On Technique for anger-control.* <br> b. *Get in the habit of noticing all of Johnny's positive behaviors.* |
| 5. Effectively weakening inappropriate behaviors | a. *Use Time-Out consistently for inappropriate temper outbursts.* <br> b. *Provide discipline in a matter-of-fact manner (no shouting).* |

# Build It to Last

## Keys to Building Strong Relationships

Unless the LORD builds the house,
its builders labor in vain.

Psalm 127:1

I don't know very much about cars. I can change a tire, jump a dead battery, add antifreeze, and in a real pinch I might be able to change the oil without killing myself (if I'm lucky). But there is one thing that I know for sure. If I get mad at my car and call it a bad name, nothing much happens. If I don't talk to my car for a couple of weeks, it still runs. I can even kick a tire and the tire will still turn. If I don't ever do anything enjoyable with my car and only use it to get to work and back, this will never have a negative effect on how well my car runs.

Do you know why? Because my car is not a person; it is a machine. Although I may have given it a cute nickname and might even be sad when I have to sell it, my car will never know my feelings. It will never respond to my interpersonal behavior. It is simply a combination of parts— a whole lot of nuts and bolts.

## Parent versus Mechanic

The same is not true for my children. If I get mad at my son and call him a name, it does affect him. If I don't talk to him for two weeks, it does impact our communication. If I punish him too harshly, he does feel it. If he hears me say something mean to Lora in anger, it will influence his view of me and possibly affect his behavior. If we never do anything fun together, it will take a toll on our relationship.

The relationships that you build with your children play a crucial role in your ability to be an effective parent. A day-care worker or school principal can use behavior management tools apart from a close relationship if they are properly trained. But to your children, you are far more than either of these. You are their mom or dad!

> The relationships that you build with your children play a crucial role in your ability to be an effective parent.

You are the one who loves them more than anyone else in this world. You are the one who prays for them on a daily basis. You saw them take their first steps. You taught them to talk. You have put bandages on their cuts and scrapes. You are their day-to-day guide through the ups and downs of growing up. You know their strengths and weaknesses. You know their accomplishments and failures. You have seen them shout with excitement, giggle with glee, and cry in embarrassment. You have been with them at their best and at their worst. You know them better than anyone else on this whole earth. You are their parent. And you can't be a parent without a relationship.

## Relationship Building

How do you build a strong relationship with your child? Let's begin by taking a quick inventory. Rate your relationship with your child on this 1 to 5 scale:

### Self Rating

| 1 | 2 | 3 | 4 | 5 |
|---|---|---|---|---|
| terrible | needs work | fair | good | excellent |

Now have your spouse or a close friend rate the relationship you have with your child. This is important because others can see things that you may not be able to. Remember, if you are married, you and your spouse are a team and you will each be more effective if you are able to give each other helpful feedback.

### Spouse's/Friend's Rating

| 1 | 2 | 3 | 4 | 5 |
|---|---|---|---|---|
| terrible | needs work | fair | good | excellent |

How did you rate your relationship with your child? How did your spouse or friend rate it? If you both rated the relationship the same way, then the ratings are probably pretty accurate. If you each rated your relationship quite differently, then find out why. What does the other person see that you do not? Spend a few minutes discussing your reasons for your evaluations. Make sure the discussion is honest and encouraging, and highlight both strengths and areas for improvement. Be open to feedback and to hearing things that you had not expected. If you are, you should be able to learn some valuable things from your discussion.

If your ratings fell into the "excellent" category, congratulations. Many of you probably fell into the "fair" and "good" categories. Some of you may have rated your relationship with your child as "needs work" or "terrible." After your discussion with your spouse or friend, you should have some ideas about why this is the case. Your goal, of course, is to move from whatever category you are currently in to the "good" or "excellent" category. For some, this will mean making only minor changes in how you interact with your child. For others, you may have to reexamine your whole style of relating. Either way, the effort you put into your relationship with your child will be well worth it. Remember, you have a limited number of years before your children are no longer children. The adult relationships between you and your children when they are grown will reflect the quality of your relationships with them *now*. There's no time to waste.

> *The adult relationships between you and your children when they are grown will reflect the quality of your relationships with them now.*

## Biblical Relationships

As you begin to build your parent-child relationships, remember that the Bible is your relationship instruction manual. God clearly identifies the ingredients necessary for healthy relationships:

> Love is patient, love is kind. It does not envy, it does not boast, it is not proud. It is not rude, it is not self-seeking, it is not easily angered, it keeps no record of wrongs. Love does not delight in evil but rejoices with the truth. It always protects, always trusts, always hopes, always perseveres.
>
> 1 Corinthians 13:4–7

> But the fruit of the Spirit is love, joy, peace, patience, kindness, goodness, faithfulness, gentleness and self-control. Against such things there is no law.
>
> Galatians 5:22–23

> Therefore, as God's chosen people, holy and dearly loved, clothe yourselves with compassion, kindness, humility, gentleness and patience. Bear with each other and forgive whatever grievances you may have against one another. Forgive as the Lord forgave you. And over all these virtues put on love, which binds them all together in perfect unity.
>
> Colossians 3:12–14

You are probably familiar with these passages that speak about how Christians are to interact with each other and with people outside of the body of Christ. If God desires that I follow these guidelines when talking to the gas station attendant down the road, shouldn't they also apply to my interaction with my own family? Definitely. In fact, it is when Christian parents apply these principles with non-family members and neglect them with their own family members that problems develop.

What, then, do these verses say to us about building strong relationships with our children? They highlight the underlying characteristics that promote close and healthy family relationships. For instance, consider how a parent who is the exact *opposite* of these verses would look:

**Parent #1**

| | |
|---|---|
| harsh | boastful |
| mean | untruthful |
| rough | impatient |
| unforgiving | blows up when angry |
| rude | easily provoked |
| holds a grudge | poor self-control |

Sound like fun? Some of these characteristics may describe the way your mother or father related to you as a child. Do any describe you at times? If so, this means you have some areas to work on. The important thing is that you are willing to diligently work on them and include them in your Parenting Plan. Remember, these are traits and behaviors that may be keeping you from being closer to your children. Let's reverse the list now and take a look at how God *would* like us to relate to our children:

**Parent #2**

| | |
|---|---|
| compassionate | humble |
| kind | truthful |
| gentle | patient |
| forgiving | expresses anger appropriately |
| respectful | slow to anger |
| forgets wrongs | shows self-control |

Let me ask you a question. Which parent would *you* rather have? Whom would *you* rather talk to about problems at school? With whom would *you* rather go to a football game or museum? Of whom would *you* rather ask embarrassing questions about sex or drugs? With whom would *you* rather go for a car ride? To whom would *you* rather admit a mistake? Whom would *you* rather have help you with a school project or introduce to your friends?

God does not demand that we be perfect. However, neither is he satisfied if we complacently allow our faults to persist. We must make every effort to become more like Parent #2 than Parent #1, striving to be gentle, patient, even-tempered, forgiving, and firm yet fair. Our lives must be guided by biblical principles and our behavior characterized by godly living.

An old saying claims, "True religion starts at home." God wants to work through you in the lives of your children. He wants your children to embrace him as their Father. You play an incredibly important role in this process. Your children will be better able to comprehend a close relationship with a loving heavenly parent if they experience close relationships with loving, earthly parents. If we truly want to be effective and influential Christian parents, then we must make every effort to build strong relationships with our children.

> *Our lives must be guided by biblical principles and our behavior characterized by godly living.*

## Relationship Building Blocks

There are many things you can do to build a strong relationship with your child. Following is a list of practical ideas for building the solid relationship you desire. This list is not profound; it is simple. However, it is often the little things that carry the most meaning for a child. In fact, here's a secret: there are no little things. Each suggestion on this list has the potential to create a memory that your child will carry for a lifetime. Why? Because even these little things take time out of your schedule, require your full attention, and communicate to your child that he or she is important enough for you to make these "sacrifices." This is why they are relationship-builders.

### Play Together in the House

Spend time playing with Legos, cars, puzzles, or other toys; reading books; coloring; cutting and pasting; playing board games or computer games; and so on. Invent your own games to play with your children. My young boys and I often have "sock wars," make a tent out of a blanket, hunt bears and monsters, play hide-and-seek, or wrestle. My two-year-old loves to pretend that he is a dog and have me pat him and throw him "sticks" to chase. All children are different and yours may enjoy activities quite different from the ones I have listed. The important thing is that you spend time playing with them on a regular basis.

### Play Together Outside of the House

Not only is getting outside to run and play fun, it is an important part of developing your child's muscles, physical coordination, hand-eye coordination, and self-confidence, as well as your relationship together. Going to the park, playing tag, blowing bubbles, playing soccer or baseball or basketball (simple versions, if needed), playing catch, going for a walk, looking at flowers, finding insects, throwing rocks into a pond, flying a kite, building a snowman—these are all great activities. And remember, the idea is not just to take your child outside and then supervise the play. Get involved! A baby-sitter can supervise your children, but no one can play with them like you can! Get your hands dirty and don't be afraid to work up a sweat.

### Show Interest in Things That Interest Your Children

Your primary interests are likely "adult" things—work, computers, adult crafts, sports, fixing things around the house, cooking, and so on. What do you think *your child* is really interested in? Matchbox cars? T-ball? Action figures? Dolls? Sports? Pretend play? Reading? Video games? Music? Make an effort to look at your child's world from his or her point of view. Show genuine interest in things that your child enjoys. Admire how "cool" a Matchbox car really looks. Get in touch with how fun it must be to learn how to hit or catch a baseball for the first time. Allow yourself to "get into" playing kitchen or other pretending games with your child. Take time to listen to some of your child's music with him or her or get involved with a hobby that your child enjoys. Make every effort possible to be at sporting events and school functions. A friend of mine used to have someone videotape his son's soccer and baseball games if he had to miss them because of work. Most importantly, he would watch the tapes the following week. His son didn't have to guess where he ranked on his father's priority list.

### Help with Homework and School Projects

Childhood is a time of learning, and school provides the academic portion of this endeavor. From the first grade on, your child will have homework to do two to five times a week. Occasionally, your child will get stuck, not understand the instructions, or need help organizing his or her work. Being available to lend a helping hand is not only a good way to help your child complete a difficult assignment, but will allow you to begin teaching your child valuable organizational, planning, and study skills. Most of all, you will provide encouragement and the unmistakable message that what is important to your child is important to you.

## Take Time to Answer Your Children's Questions

You might as well be ready. Children do not always ask questions at convenient times. Sometimes, it's appropriate for you to have them wait until you have a free minute. Other times, it means a great deal to your children if you put down your work, close your book or newspaper, or look up from your television program to talk to them. While I worked on this book at the kitchen table, there were countless times when my two sons asked me to look at something, or to get them some juice, or any of a million other things. I do mean countless. While I wasn't absolutely perfect in my responses, I can say that more often than not I stopped working and talked with them. Sometimes, I simply reminded them that I was working and could play with them later. Other times, I took short breaks and played with them on the floor. Occasionally, I let them sit on my lap and type letters or "paint" on the computer. In other instances, I took the time to scroll through my screensaver program with both of them sitting on my lap and watched them look with amazement at the various images on the screen. I probably could have gotten more work done than I did. But I wouldn't have done it any other way.

## Respond with Care When Your Child Is Upset

Your child's concerns may seem trivial or silly in an "adult" world. But to your child, they are very real and very important. When your child is upset about something, take a second to remind yourself that, no matter what the issue may be, if your child is upset or concerned about it, then it must be important to him or her. And if it is important to your child, it is important to you. Try to put yourself in your child's shoes and communicate through your words, tone of voice, and body language that you really care.

### Tell Your Children That You Love Them

This may sound obvious. There are some of you, however, who never had a parent regularly tell you that you were deeply loved. So this behavior doesn't come automatically to you. Lora and I both make it a point to tell our children that we love them on a regular, if not daily, basis. Sometimes they hear it more than once a day. As a result, I have no doubt that our children know that their parents love them very much. We've made it almost impossible for them *not* to know! As your children move into their preadolescent years, you may need to be more selective as to when you throw out an "I love you," and go easy on the hugs in front of the main school entrance. But you can still let your child know that you love him or her. Drop them an occasional note or be creative and make up a secret signal or code (e.g., thumbs up) known only to you and your children that you can use to communicate the fact that you love them.

> I have no doubt that our children know that their parents love them very much. We've made it almost impossible for them not to know!

### Address Misbehavior in a Firm but Loving Manner

Part of being a parent is setting and enforcing family rules. Hopefully, these rules will be reasonable and well planned. But you are the "enforcer" and everybody knows it. Your children *expect* you to enforce the rules. In fact, they count on you to do so. Let's face it, they're not going to do it. So, it's up to you.

Effective discipline, however, does not have to be harsh, threatening, or demeaning. In fact, these things *reduce* the effectiveness of your discipline as well as wreak havoc on your relationship with your child. If your response to your child's misbehavior tends to be one of disproportionate, intense, or shaming anger, then you are damaging your relationship with your child by the way you are choosing to respond! You are also teaching your child to *avoid* you the next time he or she has made a serious mistake and needs godly guidance or someone to talk to. How tragic! While experiencing feelings of anger and frustration is a built-in part of being a parent, you can choose to respond to misbehavior in a constructive way that honors your relationship and builds it instead of in a destructive way that dishonors and destroys one of your most prized possessions. Make it a goal for your child to be able to leave every discipline experience without ever having reason to doubt your love or respect for him or her.

### Be Willing to Apologize to Your Children

There will be times when you will blow it. Whether you express your angry feelings inappropriately, jump to an incorrect conclusion, speak disrespectfully to your child, act inconsiderately, or any of a thousand other possible wrongs, it will happen. When it happens you can try to cover it up or you can apologize to your child. If you try to cover it up, you lose in three ways. First, you lose credibility with your child because both of you know that your relationship has been violated. It is impossible to hide an elephant under a throw rug. Second, your relationship will be weakened because you have damaged it and are not willing to properly restore it by asking forgiveness as God has instructed you to do. Third, you are missing a wonderful opportunity to model for your child a humble and godly spirit that is willing to admit wrongdoing and seek reconciliation. Instead, you are showing your child how to slowly grow insensitive to God's voice and are communicating that it is acceptable to damage relationships in order to save personal pride.

On the other hand, if you are willing to apologize to your children when you blow it, this will build your credibility as a parent, help to restore and strengthen your relationship together, and provide a living example of how God wants wrongs to be handled. It doesn't get any better than that. I can tell you from experience that it can be humbling to ask your child for forgiveness and to be painfully reminded of your own fallibility. However, the joy and restoration that come from following God's plan for relationships and the knowledge that you have modeled appropriate relationship behavior for your child are rewards that far outweigh the temporary pain of demonstrating humility.

### Include Your Children in Your Activities Whenever Possible

Another nice way to build your relationship with your children is to include them in your activities. This may involve things such as them going with you to pick up something from the office, going grocery shopping, fixing the car, or any other activities that would lend themselves to having your child come along. For example, I try to jog on an irregular basis, and I have found that my younger son *loves* coming along for the ride in our jogging stroller (and I get a better workout), while my older son enjoys riding alongside me on his bicycle. As your children get older, they may be less inclined to join you in such activities (particularly in a jogging stroller!), but invite them as often as possible. Younger children will most likely find it fun and exciting to join mom or dad in an "adult" task. If you want to really score a home run, make the activity fun by stopping for a coke or doing something fun after you are through.

### Teach Your Child about God

There are several ways to teach your child about God. We will discuss three of them here. First, if your child is in the stage of liking to read books, make sure that some of the books being read contain biblical themes. There are also many good Bibles for toddlers and children and an increasing selection of Christian videos and music suitable for all ages that teach children about God. Participate in these activities with your child and let them be springboards for discussion about the content of the songs, books, or videos.

Second, take time to pray together. Whether this includes nightly prayers, giving thanks for meals, or spontaneous prayers in appropriate situations, praying together communicates that talking to God is an important part of your personal and family life. Try to provide a mix of you praying silently while your child prays out loud and allowing him or her to pray silently while hearing you pray. This type of modeling teaches your child to pray and gives you a wonderful opportunity to grow closer by sharing your personal thanks, concerns, and needs before God.

Another way to teach your child about God is to be open to opportunities to discuss biblical ideas and themes with your child. If you are looking, you will find that they present themselves regularly. The idea is not to become proficient at giving your child mini-sermons, but to naturally engage him or her in thinking about how God is a part of his or her life (and a part of yours). As a general rule, make these discussions relatively brief. We want them to be enjoyable and thought provoking, not reminiscent of a sermon that has lasted too long. When walking outside, you can talk about how God made nature (e.g., the leaves, the animals, the universe, etc.) in all of its incredible wonder. If someone is sad or discouraged, you can think together about how to comfort that person as God would like. While driving in the car you can discuss the many positive benefits of obeying God in various ways and the negative consequences that come when God's principles are ignored. Through books, videos, discussions, prayer, and everyday situations, let your relationship with your child be sprinkled with regular reminders about the reality, wonder, and goodness of God.

> Let your relationship with your child be sprinkled with regular reminders about the reality, wonder, and goodness of God.

### Schedule One-on-One Times for You and Your Child

This is a great idea if you keep it realistic. It can also become more challenging the more children you have. However, it can be done if you put your mind, and weekly planner, to work. Try to schedule one-on-one time with your child on a regular basis. It may be going out to breakfast once a month. It may be spending thirty minutes playing your child's favorite game together on a Saturday. The activity itself is not the main point, although it should be enjoyable for your child. The main point is that this time will be *regular* and that it is one-on-one time—just you and your child. You should end up having a lot of fun and you may find that some meaningful discussions will emerge during these times as well. One thing is certain. You will be communicating in a powerful way that your child is important to you.

### Spend Time Together as a Family

In my work as a psychologist, one of the questions I routinely ask children during my first session with them is, "What do you like about your family?" The answer that I get most often is, "We do fun things together." This does not mean that you have to take out a second mortgage on your house in order to buy a boat or go to Disneyland for a family vacation every winter. Fun does not have to be expensive. *It means spending time together.* We bought a family pass to the zoo this year and I can tell you where every animal in that zoo is located—and the year is not even half over yet! Many children like riding bicycles on bike trails, going to parks, playing extended Monopoly games (a true test of parental love), and many, many other things. Bring a camera along and make some memories. If you need ideas for things to do, ask your child. Ask other parents what fun things they do with their children. You can also find several books that contain many ideas for fun family activities. Years later, these will be your most precious memories.

Spending time together may require scheduling your family time well in advance. Our family has recently declared every Saturday night to be "family night." We decide on a fun activity for the evening and also include a time for talking together about how everyone is doing or what has been going on that week. We may talk about how to solve a problem, how to show someone that you love them, or any topic that seems appropriate for the week. Discussion about God always seems to naturally weave its way into our conversations and occasionally we may include a short devotional time in our family night. These are times that are focused on enjoying each other, building our relationships, and growing together as a family that loves God. We all love these nights and I find that they are often the highlight of my busy week. As we continue to have our family nights, I am becoming more and more aware of the important role they play in helping our family to develop a strong sense of unity and commitment to each other.

### Learn to Enjoy Your Child

Childhood passes all too quickly. Take time to stop and realize how wonderful your child is and how wonderful is the God who made him or her. Don't let the worries and pressures of life rob you of your perspective on what is really important. Remind yourself of the positive characteristics that your child is developing. Think about the cute, innocent, hilarious, and spontaneous ways that your child brings joy into your life every day. Take a minute to thank God for your child and enjoy the privilege of being a parent.

## Communication

I cannot talk about building healthy relationships without saying a few words about communication. Communication is a central part of relationship building. Without it, you won't have a relationship. Unfortunately, this is what was beginning to happen between one mother and daughter that I met a few years ago.

"She never *listens* to me!" the eleven-year-old girl complained with a pained look on her face, as she slumped in the chair in my office. "What do you mean I never listen?" quickly interrupted the mother. "All I do is listen to you. Why, Doc, we're like the best of friends. We talk and talk. She tells me what is going on, how things are going at school, with boys, you know, everything. There's nothing that she can't feel comfortable telling me . . ." As her mother carried on, the girl just sat there, rolling her eyes, with a resigned look on her face. Lots of words; no communication.

### Listening to Your Children

The two basic components of communication, talking and listening, are both very important and require lots of practice. Let's first look at how you can listen to your children in a way that will help build a healthy relationship.

*Communication is a central part of relationship building.*

1. *Temporarily stop whatever you are doing.* Put down your book, look away from the TV, or look up from your work. Then look at your child, make eye contact, and shift your body toward him or her if possible. The three or four seconds that it takes to do this says one thing loud and clear: "What you have to say is important to me because *you* are important to me!"

2. *As a rule, listen more and speak less.* Your goal is to understand your child and to help your child learn to express his or her thoughts and feelings. So make it a point to give your child time to finish what he or she is saying before you jump in. Add your own comments only *after* you have listened thoroughly.

3. *Repeat what your child says, using your own words.* To make sure that you have listened correctly and to communicate to your child that you are listening, paraphrase

your child's comments and repeat the paraphrase to your child. For example, if your child says, "There's nothing to do," you might say, "You're having a hard time staying busy." This type of response is great for prompting further interaction. It may feel kind of awkward at first, but believe me, this is a wonderful way to really listen to your child.

4. *Identify and state the feelings that your child expresses.* Listen for the feelings (e.g., hurt, happy, upset, frustrated, excited, worried, etc.) beneath your child's words. Pay attention to your child's choice of words, tone of voice, and body language. Then make your best guess as to what your child is probably feeling right now. Tentatively offer your guess about what your child may be feeling. For example, if your child says, "I can't do this!" you might say, "You sound really frustrated right now." Or if your child complains, "That's not fair!" you could respond with, "My guess is that you might feel a little angry about this." If your guess is incorrect, your child will let you know. If your guess is correct, your child will feel like you are really tuning in to what he or she is feeling. Either way, your child will appreciate your careful listening and you will be communicating that what he or she has to say is important to you.

5. *Make every effort to really understand your child.* Remind yourself that what your child has to say is important. Listen with the intent of learning about your child and understanding his or her thoughts and world. There's nothing that breathes life into a relationship like the experience of being listened to and valued. If you want to increase the chances that your child will want to talk to you as a teenager, make sure that you are a good listener now.

### Talking with Your Children

The general guideline for talking with your children is this: Talk to your children the way that you would like others to talk to you. Sound familiar? Here are some helpful tips that you can begin to use right away.

1. *Look at your child.* If you are involved in an activity, put it down and look at your child. Don't make a habit of talking to your child from underneath a magazine or with your eyes glued to the television set. Just as looking at your child is important when you are listening, it is also important when you are talking. This behavior has *"You are important!"* written all over it and will help increase the chances that your child will be listening.

2. *Keep it simple.* Use language and words your child is familiar with and can understand. No one likes to be talked down to. Without being condescending, speak to your child on his or her level, going into only as much detail as your child can handle.

3. *Be honest.* Children value and learn from their parents' honesty. Give honest yet age-appropriate answers to their questions. Feel free to use correct names for physical parts of the body, and if you don't know something, say so. Tell your child that you can find the answer together and then turn that into a relationship-building activity.

4. *Communicate with warmth and respect.* As you talk with your children, make sure your choice of words and tone of voice never drown out the value you place on them. Even when handling challenging situations, always communicate with your children in a way that conveys your respect for them and upholds their unique place of importance on your priority list. I firmly believe that you can effectively handle even the most difficult situation while still treating your children in a respectful manner. Take inventory of how you give commands, make requests, express your frustration, and make playful comments to your children. Remember, apples usually don't fall too far from the tree!

5. *Be encouraging.* Talking with you and listening to you should be an enjoyable and rewarding experience for your child. As much as possible, be positive and encouraging in your interactions. Be the kind of parent that your children will want to talk to!

## Make a Plan

Think seriously about the steps you need to take to build a strong, healthy relationship with your children. If you need to work on controlling your temper, being more respectful, increasing your patience, improving your communication, or any of the other items listed earlier, ask someone close to you to hold you accountable for making these changes. Perhaps you and your spouse could each pick one area in which to improve and agree to help each other by providing loving and honest feedback along with plenty of encouragement. If you are a single parent, you can ask a close friend to regularly check in with you regarding the relationship improvements you'd like to make. Be sure to set regular check-in dates so that you can find out how you are doing. For some of you, it could be that meeting with a pastoral counselor or Christian therapist may be a good first step in discovering how to remove the obstacles that block your relationships with your children.

Everyone can improve somehow in the way we relate to our children. To get started, answer the questions below:

**Q.** *What are three things that I can improve in my relationship with my child?*

Example: *Be more patient.*
*Improve our communication.*
*Spend more time together.*

_____

_____

_____


***Q.*** *What is the first step I must take to make each of these improvements a reality?*

Example:  *Silently count to ten and tell myself to calm down when I start feeling angry.*

*Make sure that I have fully listened before I begin to offer advice.*

*Spend thirty minutes playing after dinner on Monday, Wednesday, and Friday.*

_____

_____

_____


***Q.*** *Whom will I ask to keep me accountable for making these changes?*

Example:  *spouse or close friend*

_____

_____

_____

You should now have some practical ideas for improving your relationships with your children. Take the time now to complete this section of your Parenting Plan in appendix A. There are not too many things in life as important as your relationships with your children. Do all that you can to make your relationships ones that will guide and inspire your children toward God instead of ones that deter the development of a strong relationship with their heavenly Father. Your children need healthy relationships with you. They desire that very much (regardless of what they may say!). Build your relationship with your children according to God's plan as you strive to be the best parent that you can be.

# three

# They Noticed That?

## *Understanding the Influence of Your Behavior*

> Follow my example, as I follow the example of Christ.
>
> 1 Corinthians 11:1

Pretend that you have never seen a volleyball match in your life. Can you imagine how difficult it would be to learn the game if your instructor could not use his hands or show you any of the equipment used in the game, such as the ball or the net? Now consider how much easier it would be if your instructor could use his hands and show you the equipment, and if you were even allowed to watch a game of volleyball being played.

A picture *is* worth a thousand words, and modeling is one of the most effective methods of teaching available. When you "model" a behavior, you provide students with an example, or a model, of what they are to do. This visual picture aids tremendously in the process of learning a new behavior.

Josh Billings adds a twist to Proverbs 22:6: "Train up a child in the way he should go . . . and go there yourself

51

every now and then!" Whether you are aware of it or not, you model many behaviors for your children every day. Every hour. Every minute. In every happy moment and in every angry moment, you are the show and your children are the audience—and they don't miss a thing. This thought was sobering for me when I learned that Lora was pregnant with our first son. I realized that from that time on there would be a little pair of eyes watching everything I did, perhaps even idolizing me. I became aware that I could no longer let things slip when I was mad, make inappropriate jokes, or spend a few extra seconds viewing a questionable show while channel surfing. I was about to become the teacher and my life the lesson.

> "Train up a child in the way he should go . . . and go there yourself every now and then."

## Actions Speak Louder Than Words

It is well established that listeners more readily believe what a speaker does than what a speaker says. So if you say you are happy but look very sad, most people will believe your actions rather than your words. In the same way, children learn far more from how their parents behave than from what their parents say.

One day our whole family was outdoors and I was at work mowing the front yard. Before long, I rounded a turn and caught a glimpse of our youngest son out of the corner of my eye. There he was with his black and red plas-

tic lawnmower, following along beside me with a very determined look on his face as he "mowed" the sidewalk. I
immediately smiled and felt honored as I watched him
work so hard to emulate his dad. I had not told him to pull
out his lawnmower, but there he was, doing exactly what
he watched his father do. Suddenly a thought hit me that
nearly stopped me in my tracks. If my son made this much
of an effort to imitate me while I engaged in a behavior as
trivial as mowing the lawn, how much would he attempt
to duplicate my behavior in the areas of life that really
count?

Think about all of the things that your parents said to
you when you were a child. How many *exact* statements do
you remember from those days? One, maybe two? Consid-
ering all the thousands of state-
ments your parents made to
you during those eighteen to
twenty years, that is a pretty
small percentage. However,
most of us remember *very
clearly* the kind of people our
parents were and how they
acted toward us. We observed
their marriage. We saw how
they responded to pressure and
how they handled problems.
We were keenly aware of how
they expressed their feelings.
We saw how often they spent
time in prayer or reading the
Scripture. We noticed if they
acted one way in church and
another at home.

> Listeners
> more read-
> ily believe
> what a
> speaker
> does than
> what a
> speaker
> says.

We don't remember all of these things because our parents told them to us. We remember them because we saw
them firsthand hundreds of times. Our children are watch-

ing us with the same openness, the same tenacity, the same ability to learn. What they learn will be up to us.

The behavior we model for our children affects them in two primary areas: their immediate day-to-day behavior and their ongoing development as persons. On a daily basis children imitate behaviors they see others do. So if you tend to shout when you are angry, don't be surprised if your children develop a habit of shouting or throwing tantrums when they are angry. If you often leave messes around the house, it shouldn't shock you if your kids resist cleaning up their toys. If you rarely talk about God or pray at home, don't be surprised if your children do not learn to value their own spiritual relationship. Other factors also affect these behaviors, but the behavior that you model will not go unnoticed.

If you model negative behaviors for your child over long periods of time, they will eventually become a regular part of your child's behavior. Such behaviors may be difficult to change when your child is older. If you try to persuade an eleven-year-old boy to talk more respectfully while his parents model poor communication habits on a daily basis, he will see no reason to change his behavior. "If Mom and Dad can do it, why can't I?" will be his response. The pattern of poor communication skills he is learning will negatively affect his relationships and he will miss precious opportunities as a child to learn healthier ways of communicating with others.

## Biblical Modeling

Paul knew the value of modeling. He exhorted the believers in Corinth to follow his example: "Follow my example, as I follow the example of Christ" (1 Cor. 11:1). Paul encouraged others to watch and learn as he did his best to model godly behavior for them.

What type of behavior does God want us to model for our children? Let's look at a passage that gives us some ideas:

> Therefore each of you must put off falsehood and speak truthfully to his neighbor, for we are all members of one body. "In your anger do not sin": Do not let the sun go down while you are still angry, and do not give the devil a foothold. He who has been stealing must steal no longer, but must work, doing something useful with his own hands, that he may have something to share with those in need.
>
> Do not let any unwholesome talk come out of your mouths, but only what is helpful for building others up according to their needs, that it may benefit those who listen. And do not grieve the Holy Spirit of God, with whom you were sealed for the day of redemption. Get rid of all bitterness, rage and anger, brawling and slander, along with every form of malice. Be kind and compassionate to one another, forgiving each other, just as in Christ God forgave you. Be imitators of God, therefore, as dearly beloved children and live a life of love, just as Christ loved us and gave himself up for us as a fragrant offering and sacrifice to God.
>
> But among you there must not be even a hint of sexual immorality, or of any kind of impurity, or of greed, because these are improper for God's holy people. Nor should there be obscenity, foolish talk or coarse joking, which are out of place, but rather thanksgiving. For of this you can be sure: No immoral, impure or greedy person—such a man is an idolater—has any inheritance in the kingdom of Christ and of God.
>
> Ephesians 4:25–5:5

This is no small order. We are called to honesty, communication that builds others up, healthy expression of anger, forgiveness, a balanced view of material possessions, and much more. The passages we discussed regarding healthy relationships in chapter 1 also describe important behaviors God intends for us to model for our children. In fact, he is counting on us to do this, for our modeling these behaviors is an *essential* part of how our children will learn biblical values and godly behaviors. Remember, modeling means teaching, and you are the teacher God has placed in your children's lives.

As I write this section, I cannot help but think of my parents. While I was growing up our family, much like yours perhaps, went through some hard times. Financial difficulties, marital tension, rebellious teenagers—we had it all.

> Our model-
> ing these
> behaviors is
> an essential
> part of how
> our children
> will learn
> biblical values
> and godly
> behaviors.

I can remember times when the money simply wasn't there and my parents had to take jobs they were overqualified for just to make ends meet. I vividly recall times when the strain of personal and family issues brought tension into my parents' marriage. I can still see the look of frustration, at times mixed with desperation, on their faces as they labored over how to best respond to the most challenging aspects of teenage behavior. Over time, I was able to watch my father and my mother work through each of these challenges and many more in a manner demonstrating their authentic faith in God. I marveled at the way my father stayed firm in his belief that God would honor his promises, even though external circumstances said otherwise. In my mother, I saw a remarkable mixture of tenacity and compassion that would draw little attention to her own hurt but would grieve for the wounds of others. From both of my parents I learned the value of hard work, the meaning of commitment, and the sacrificial nature of parental love. I often wonder if I will ever develop the same level of integrity and faith in God that I have seen modeled for me over the years. I know, however, that the path toward that kind of integrity and faith has been made easier for me because my parents traveled it first.

## A Plan of Action

It's time now for a little proactive thinking. Make a list of the characteristics and traits that you would like to see your children develop. You may include characteristics such as loving God, honesty, kindness, integrity, forgiving others, being flexible, making thoughtful decisions, self-control, perseverance, having a good sense of humor, being unselfish, humility, and so on.

In each of these areas, determine the quality of that trait in your life. Honesty counts here. For each trait, indicate either good, fair, or poor.

| Desired Characteristic | Rating in Parent's Life | | |
| --- | --- | --- | --- |
| | good | fair | poor |
| _____ | ☐ | ☐ | ☐ |
| _____ | ☐ | ☐ | ☐ |
| _____ | ☐ | ☐ | ☐ |
| _____ | ☐ | ☐ | ☐ |
| _____ | ☐ | ☐ | ☐ |
| _____ | ☐ | ☐ | ☐ |

This is not only a list of traits that you would like your *children* to develop, but is also a list of traits that need to be present in *your* life if you want to be most effective at helping your children develop these characteristics. Your self-rating gives you a rough indicator of how you are doing with these behaviors right now and an idea of which characteristics you need to work on.

If your child is displaying problem behaviors that concern you, remember the baseball diamond. First, make sure that your relationship is where it should be. That is the pitcher's mound. Then, to pass first base, list your child's problem behavior and rate your behavior in the same area.

| Problem Behavior | Parent's Behavior | | |
| --- | --- | --- | --- |
| | good | fair | poor |
| _____ | ☐ | ☐ | ☐ |
| _____ | ☐ | ☐ | ☐ |
| _____ | ☐ | ☐ | ☐ |
| _____ | ☐ | ☐ | ☐ |
| _____ | ☐ | ☐ | ☐ |
| _____ | ☐ | ☐ | ☐ |

For example, if your child is having a difficult time learning to properly express her angry feelings and control her temper, rate yourself on how you express angry feelings and control your temper. If this is an area with which you also have a difficult time, you might rate yourself with a "fair" or "poor" rating.

This doesn't mean that your behavior is single-handedly responsible for your child's temper tantrums. There may be many other factors that play a role, including your child's temperament and age, inappropriate anger expression being accidentally reinforced, or underdeveloped anger-control skills. However, your behavior likely contributes to your child's temper problems, and continued displays of poor anger-control on your part will only make it more difficult for your child to learn to control her anger more appropriately. Changes will probably be needed in several areas, and the way you handle your anger will be one of them.

As we bring this chapter to a close, identify changes that you need to make in your interpersonal and family behavior to model positive behavior for your children. List behaviors clearly and specifically. I do not know of any parents, myself included, who could not either regularly or occasionally make some improvements in the behavior that they model for their children.

**Changes I Will Make to Model Positive Behavior**

_____        _____

_____        _____

_____        _____

_____        _____

_____        _____

Changing behavior can be difficult. Choose someone to help you make the changes that you would like to make in your behavior. It may be helpful to work on one behavior at a time and to check in with your accountability partner on a regular basis to see how you are doing. The behavior you model will have a lasting impact on your child's development during the childhood and teenage years. Remember, changes don't happen overnight and you are bound to make mistakes along the way. But as long as your attempts to model appropriate biblical behavior are an outgrowth of an authentic and growing relationship with God, you are on the right track.

We have now covered the first base of our baseball diamond. You should have many ideas about how to more effectively model appropriate behavior. Write them into your Parenting Plan in appendix A. Once you have done that, move on to second base, where we will discuss how to effectively teach your children *exactly* what you want them to do.

# Let's Do This Instead

## How to Teach Your Children What You Want Them to Do

Train a child in the way he should go,
and when he is old he will not turn from it.

Proverbs 22:6

After we have examined the quality of our relationships with our children and the behavior that we are modeling for them, the next two steps involve teaching and strengthening appropriate behaviors. But why is it so important to focus on increasing appropriate behaviors? Why not move right into reducing negative behaviors with discipline?

## The Road to Effective Teaching

Many inappropriate behaviors continue to occur because your child has never been taught a reasonable set of alter-

61

native behaviors. Many of us spend so much time and energy focusing on our children's negative behavior that we never take the time to consider whether we have taught them what to do *instead* of the misbehavior. And often, we have not. If you attempt to decrease your child's misbehavior but neglect to teach appropriate replacement behaviors, your plan gets out of balance. You are telling your child what *not* to do instead of teaching him or her what to do. If you don't teach your child how you would like him or her to respond in a certain situation, your child is likely to respond with the same negative behavior the next time the situation arises.

For example, if Susan has a difficult time controlling her temper, you should help her develop a practical set of anger-control steps she can use in difficult situations. You can review and practice these steps with her to help her learn them and to increase the likelihood that she will actually use them when necessary. Then, when Susan uses her new steps you can provide her with plenty of positive reinforcement to help strengthen this new behavior. Just as it is easier to learn a new game by first reading the instructions, seeing the game pieces, and taking a few trial runs, children will be far more likely to display an appropriate behavior if you take the time to teach them *exactly* what that behavior is and how to do it.

Another reason desired behaviors are not seen more often is that they have starved to death from a lack of positive reinforcement. When your child listens the first time, appropriately expresses angry feelings, shares a toy, or behaves in some other positive way, how do you typically respond? You may breathe a grateful sigh of relief that a problem situation didn't just break out and do your best not to upset the tranquility of this rare and precious moment. Or you may simply be so busy with other demands on your time that you don't even notice when your child has behaved in a particularly positive manner. Most of us have trained ourselves to be on the lookout for only one thing—negative behavior! When that occurs, we immediately respond to it with our full and utmost attention. Unfortunately, that means your child's negative behavior gets your attention while positive behavior is ignored.

If you don't provide positive feedback when your child behaves appropriately, you miss a wonderful opportunity to strengthen an appropriate behavior and increase the frequency with which it occurs. Kids don't magically learn to behave nicely. They learn to behave appropriately by coming to the conclusion that positive behaviors usually bring positive consequences. And this is a lesson you can help them learn by wisely controlling the consequences that follow their behavior. That means making sure that positive consequences consistently follow desired behaviors. If you consistently do this, you'll be shocked at the difference positive reinforcement can make.

*Kids don't magically learn to behave nicely.*

## The Place to Start

As we have discussed, Scripture has much to say to parents. We are to inspire our children to love the Lord and teach them the value of honoring God. We are to love them as we love ourselves and relate to them in a respectful and godly manner. The Bible clearly outlines our responsibility to teach our children to behave appropriately:

> Fix these words of mine in your hearts and minds; tie them as symbols on your hands and bind them on your foreheads.

Teach them to your children, talking about them when you sit at home and when you walk along the road, when you lie down and when you get up. Write them on the doorframes of your houses and on your gates, so that your days and the days of your children may be many in the land that the LORD swore to give your forefathers, as many as the days that the heavens are above the earth.

*Deuteronomy 11:18–21*

He said to them, "Take to heart all the words I have solemnly declared to you this day, so that you may command your children to obey carefully all the words of this law."

*Deuteronomy 32:46*

Train a child in the way he should go,
    and when he is old he will not turn from it.

*Proverbs 22:6*

Children, obey your parents in everything, for this pleases the Lord.

*Colossians 3:20*

He must manage his own family well and see that his children obey him with proper respect.

*1 Timothy 3:4*

We are to teach our children about God, about biblical values, about relationships, about integrity and character, and about the consequences that follow behavior—both positive and negative. But how do we go about this teaching process? As you might guess, the answer to that question includes using *every* part of our baseball diamond: building meaningful relationships with our children, modeling appropriate and godly behavior, teaching our children desired behaviors, rewarding those behaviors, and using effective discipline techniques when inappropriate behaviors occur.

## Teach Them What to Do

Now that you understand why it is important to start by increasing your child's positive behavior, we can move on to how you go about doing this. I'll introduce you to two methods for teaching a child appropriate behavior. The first is what I call the Detour Method. I call it the Detour Method because that is exactly what it can be for your child. It gives your child an alternative route—a detour — around the negative behavior. Just as a detour takes you to your desired destination while helping you avoid hazardous road conditions, using the Detour Method provides your child with a set of alternative behaviors that will help him or her avoid the negative consequences that are waiting just around the corner. Here's how it works:

---

### The Detour Method

**D**ecide exactly what you want your child to do.

**e**

**T**each your child the new behavior by practicing it together.

**o**

**U**

**R**eview and rehearse this new behavior with your child, using practice sessions and quizzes that are short and fun.

---

Decide. Teach. Review. This is a great way to teach your child a new behavior. The steps need to happen in this order because before you can review a behavior, your child has to know how to do it. And before you can teach your child how to do it, you have to decide *exactly* what you want your child to do.

### Decide

Do you remember when I said that you are the primary teacher in your child's life? Well, warm up your piece of chalk and bad jokes, because now it's time to do some teaching. Instead of thinking about what you want your child to stop doing, I want you to think about what you would like your child to start doing! If you don't want five-year-old Sarah to hit, what would you like her to do instead? If you don't want her to run away from you at the grocery store, what *do* you want her to do? If you don't want her to scream when she is angry, how should she express her anger? Exactly what do you want her to do if another child takes her toy, or hits her first? By the way, if you are having a tough time with these questions, think about how difficult it may be for Sarah to figure out the answers.

The first step of the Detour Method is to decide exactly what you would like your child to do. Here's how you get started. Get a piece of paper and a pencil and list three or four problem behaviors. Then next to each one, write down simple replacement behaviors for your child. Below are examples of problem behaviors and replacement behaviors we might identify for Sarah.

| Problem Behaviors | Replacement Behaviors |
| --- | --- |
| 1. Hitting when mad | a. Ignore the behavior. |
| | b. Move somewhere else. |
| | c. Say, "Please stop bothering me." |
| | d. Get help from parents or teacher. |
| 2. Not listening to parents | a. Just do it. (Say, "Okay, Mom.") |
| | b. Ask questions or make comments in a nice voice. |
| | c. If the answer is no, then just do it. |
| | d. Talk about it later, if needed. |

As you decide upon the replacement behaviors, picture yourself in your child's shoes. How would you feel if someone grabbed something that you were using? What is a practical solution that would be helpful to you if you were five years old? Include older children in the determination of replacement behaviors. The more input they have into the plan, the more likely they will be to accept it. Remember, the solution must be in a simple step-by-step format.

> *Once your child learns the replacement behavior, he or she will do the problem behavior less frequently!*

Picture your child doing these steps. Do you think he or she can do them? Do the steps make sense? Are they practical and realistic or are they too complicated? If you have any doubts, simplify them. You can always make the plan more sophisticated later. We want your child to succeed at this skill. The simpler the plan is, the better chance that he or she will do it! The more often your child does it, the better chance that he or she will really learn it. Once your child learns and consistently practices the replacement behavior, he or she will do the problem behavior less frequently!

### Teach

Once you have decided exactly what you want your child to do, you must teach him or her how to use the new steps. For best results, begin with one behavior. It can be too confusing if you try to address several new behaviors at once. If you have decided, for example, that you would like Sarah to control her anger, tell her that you are going to help her learn to do this. Take the opportunity to talk about why this is an important behavior, pointing out both the benefits of the behavior (e.g., obedience to God's Word, effective problem solving, improved relationships) and the negative con-

sequences of the inappropriate behavior (e.g., failure to follow God's Word, additional problems, further trouble).

Next, explain and demonstrate the steps to Sarah. For example, if you are working on a replacement behavior for hitting, identify situations in which this behavior happens (e.g.,
someone grabs Sarah's toy). Pretend that you are Sarah and
have her grab your toy. Then, respond as she *usually* does by
pretending to hit. Briefly discuss what the usual consequences
for that behavior would be. Next role-play the situation again,
and this time, use the steps for the replacement behavior.
When you've finished have Sarah identify the consequences
(positive this time) of this new behavior. You will be modeling the appropriate behavior for her, allowing her to watch
you and making it easier for her to learn. Make sure she understands what to do and then have her do it, with you taking her toy. Have Sarah first respond in her usual manner and
then respond with the new behavior, making sure to practice all of the steps. As Sarah makes an effort and eventually
completes the replacement behavior, give her plenty of positive feedback. If you provide plenty of enthusiasm and attention, this practice should be quite fun for both of you. As
you go through the steps for the replacement behavior, be
open to any ideas Sarah may have about how to use the steps.
She may come up with a helpful step that you didn't think
of. If you can incorporate any of Sarah's ideas into the steps,
she will be that much more invested in using them.

### Review

Finally, review and rehearse the steps with your child to
help him or her learn them well. If your child is old enough,
help him or her memorize the steps. Remember, keep it
fun! Make rehearsals brief and enjoyable. You want your
child to experience a sense of accomplishment and success
as he or she learns these steps. If Sarah is able to memorize
the steps, give her a sticker (or a quarter!) every time she

can state them following a pop quiz, along with plenty of positive feedback. You can give Johnny a brief quiz on the steps while riding in the car, at the dinner table, or almost anytime during the day. If you have a computer, print the steps out with a neat graphic, in a font of his choice. Let Sarah make a poster out of them and tape them to her bedroom wall if she wants to. Be creative! Then several times a week, during positive times, rehearse the steps with your child using "real-life" situations, first modeling the steps if you need to. Soon, your child should have them down cold.

### Put It Together

To help you get started, here are some examples of steps for a few common problems:

*Telephone interruptions.* There's nothing like you getting on the telephone to turn your child into a human magnet! Steps for preventing telephone interruptions might include the following:

- Wait until mom or dad is finished talking.
- If it is important, say, "Excuse me," in a nice voice.
- Then wait quietly for mom or dad to respond.

Once you have come up with your steps, stage some rehearsals. Pick up the phone and pretend that you are talking to someone. If you really want to have some fun, have a friend call you just so that you can practice! For this behavior, you might also want to teach your child when it is important to interrupt, such as when someone is hurt or in an emergency situation. Remember to give your child lots of positive feedback as she performs the steps.

*Wandering at the mall.* If your child has a habit of darting off every time you pause to look in a store window, you must decide exactly what you would like your child to do at the mall. Then go to the mall to practice, preferably when it is not too crowded. Talk about an excuse for going shopping! Once you are there, review and practice the steps with your child. Possible steps include:

- Stay in the "zone" (the walking zone).
- When mom says, "Stop," or "Red light," get back in the zone.

For example, if you want your child to stay within a five- to ten-foot distance in front of you or to the side, show him exactly how far this is. Have him stand by you and then slowly walk away. When he is about ten feet away tell him to stop and have him look back to see how far away he is. Do this several times until he understands how far away he can go. (You can also use the game "Red Light, Green Light" for the same purpose.) Then slowly begin to walk together. As your child stays within the "walking zone," give him lots of positive feedback. Help him to feel like he is learning something important because he is! If your child steps out of the walking zone, say, "Stop" (or "Red light"), have him come back, and try again. Keep on practicing and if he makes a good effort, surprise him with an ice-cream cone.

*Sharing toys.* If your child tends to monopolize the toy supply, the following steps may be useful for her to use when someone asks her for a toy:

- If she is still using the toy, say, "I'm using it right now, but you can use it when I'm finished."
- If she would like to share, say, "Sure, you can use it." Then find something else to play with or suggest, "Why don't we play with it together?"

This is a good behavior for role-playing. Pretend that your child wants to borrow a toy from you and model both the old behavior and the new behavior. Ask your child how she feels following each. Talk together about the benefits of sharing (e.g., helps us to make friends, makes people want to share with us, pleases God). Also, point out that she does not *always* have to share and that there may be a few toys that are just hers. Practice the steps together, letting her experience how fun it is to share with someone.

*Listening to mom and dad.* This is the set of steps that I use most frequently for helping children learn to listen better to their parents. Many parents I have worked with have found them to be very useful. When asked to do something, your child can do the following:

- Just do it. (Say, "Okay, Mom.")
- Ask questions or make comments in a nice voice.
- If the answer is no, then just do it.
- Talk about it *later*, if needed.

Practice these steps in a variety of situations, especially situations where your child argues or is often noncompliant. Make a clear distinction between asking a question in a nice voice and asking one in a rude or arguing tone. It's important for your child to be able to ask a reasonable question in response to a parental request. After all, we are not raising robots, we are raising thinking children who sometimes have very good questions. Practice giving a yes answer (e.g., "Sure, you can watch for five more minutes") and a no answer (e.g., "No, Johnny, I really need you to come right now") in response to your child's question. Emphasize that your child can always talk with you later about the situation if he wants to, *after* he has done what you have asked.

*Expressing angry feelings.* If your child is learning how to express her angry feelings when another child bothers her, here are some steps that you can choose from:

- Ignore the behavior.
- Express her feelings in words by saying, "When _____, I feel _____."
- Say, "Please stop _____."
- Firmly repeat her request for the other person to stop.
- Walk away.
- Get involved in another activity.
- Get some assistance from a parent or teacher.

As usual, practice these steps by role-playing situations that often anger your child. Model the steps and then have your child practice them. You can also discuss more negative options (e.g., hitting and shouting) and the negative consequences that would follow those behaviors, contrasting them with the positive consequences that would follow using the steps.

As you can see, the steps do not have to be complicated to be effective. In fact, simple steps often work very well because they are easy to remember. Once your child has begun to learn the steps, you will have something to reward. You will also have something that you can refer him or her to (e.g., "Sarah, remember your steps!") when you see a problem situation brewing. This is a *great* way to prevent a problem from occurring in the first place! Remember, there's no one "perfect" set of steps for any behavior. Just make sure that the steps are appropriate, realistic, and within your child's capability. Then, go over the steps together and practice them in an enjoyable way. For younger children, keep it to two, three, or four steps. For older children, you can include up to five steps while still keeping it simple enough to remember.

## Problem-Solving Steps

The second way to teach children appropriate behavior is to give them a plan for effectively responding to problems or challenging situations. When faced with a problem, many children will impulsively react in a negative way because they have never learned a more effective way of handling tough situations. The replacement behavior that you want your child to learn is to stop and think before acting. Based on a very helpful problem-solving process[1], here are the steps that I use most often when teaching children how to solve problems more effectively. The first letters of the Problem-Solving Steps conveniently spell the word *steps*.

---

### Problem-Solving Steps

**S**top and state the problem
**T**hink about solutions
**E**valuate the solutions
**P**ick a solution
**S**ee if it worked

---

You can teach these Problem-Solving Steps to your child by first explaining them in simple terms. As a general rule, these steps work best with children age seven and older, as younger children may have a difficult time understanding them.

### Stop and State the Problem

This first step contains two important elements: stopping and stating. Stopping is extremely important as it will keep your child from doing or saying something inappropriate and will give him a chance to think and use the other steps. If he doesn't stop, the later steps will never have a chance to help. Good ways of stopping include mentally reminding yourself to stop and think, taking a few deep breaths, and counting from one to ten.

Stating the problem helps narrow it down and makes it more manageable to deal with. "He's such a jerk!" is not as helpful as, "I get really angry when he turns up the TV so loud that I can't hear my music." When these steps are used in a family setting, each member gets an opportunity to state the problem from his or her own perspective. A sentence that can help your child to briefly and clearly state the problem is, "When _____ happens, I feel _____, and this is a problem for me because _____."

### Think about Solutions

The next step is to think of solutions—at least four or five of them. In family therapy sessions, I often have a family think of eight to twelve possible solutions and have never yet been disappointed by their ability to successfully do so. The key is to be creative and to brainstorm any solution you might think possible. Think of ways to prevent the problem, other ways to get things accomplished, methods of rewarding desired behavior, negative consequences that would be appropriate, ways to compromise, possible replacement behaviors, how to use positive communication, and so on. Also list negative solutions, if they are something that your child might do or has done (e.g., name-calling). This gives your child a chance to contrast the consequences of positive and negative solutions. If your child chooses from just one or two possibilities, she may miss a better solution waiting around the corner.

### Evaluate the Solutions

Once your child has a list of solutions, the solutions can be evaluated. Your child should consider the pros and cons and the likely outcome of each. Give each solution a "+" or "–" rating and explain why. Some solutions may seem to solve the problem but actually only postpone it and result in a greater problem in the future. Carefully and realistically evaluate each solution as to how well it will solve the problem.

### Pick a Solution

Your child must then pick a solution or combination of solutions that he thinks will be the most effective approach to the problem. Specify exactly what will be needed for the solution to be implemented. Together with your child, try to think of any potential problems with the solution that you may have missed. If you predict problems, figure out a way to handle them by altering or adding to the solution. If your child has difficulty arriving at an effective solution, try to come up with more possible solutions, take a break and come back to the problem-solving process at a later time, or do some "research" to get some ideas from other credible sources (e.g., parents, friends, friends' parents, teachers, books, etc.). Once your child has chosen a solution he will need to specify how and when it will be put into effect.

### See If It Worked

Finally, make sure that your child learns from his problem-solving work. Every problem-solving attempt is an experiment—either the chosen solution will be effective or it will not. If the solution was effective your child should remember this for future reference. If the solution wasn't effective, he should find a better solution to try in the future. This step can be put into action by setting a date to review the solution to determine how effective it was.

### Watch It Work

It may be helpful to work through an "easy" problem together so that your child can see how the steps work. Use the acrostic to help your child remember the steps and, as always, keep your instruction fun and positive.

For example, let's observe Janet's parents addressing the problem behavior that occurs when her younger sister starts to pester her. In the past, Janet has resorted to name-calling, disrespectful speech, and occasional pushing. Her parents started by acknowledging that her sister's behavior must be very annoying to Janet: "We know, Janet, that when Lauren interrupts you and tries to tag along with you all the time, it must be *very* frustrating. However, the way you respond to her is not appropriate. Let's try these Problem-Solving Steps to see if we can find a good solution for when Lauren starts to bother you."

*Keep your instruction fun and positive.*

Having recognized her feelings and the need for a change in behavior, Janet and her parents worked through the Problem-Solving Steps together, one at a time.

### Stop and State the Problem

Janet: "When Lauren interrupts me and always tries to play with me and my friends, I feel annoyed because I would like to do a few things on my own without having her involved."

Parents: "When we see you get so angry at Lauren when she tries to get involved in your activities, we feel upset about how you handle it. Yet we know that her behavior is frustrating for you. This is a problem for us because we don't like to see you treat Lauren in a disrespectful or aggressive way and because you also end up getting into trouble for how you act toward her."

### THINK ABOUT SOLUTIONS

After stating their perspective of the problem and allowing Janet to share her viewpoint, Janet's parents turned their attention to possible solutions, seeing how many solutions Janet could come up with on her own before adding their own ideas and taking turns thinking of them together. Here is a partial list of solutions for Janet (see if you can add your own!):

1. Push Lauren away.
2. Tell Lauren (respectfully) that you would like to play alone right now. Repeat this statement if necessary.
3. Call Lauren a mean name (e.g., a brat).
4. Get up and go to your room to play.
5. Have mom and dad tell Lauren that Janet can play by herself sometimes.
6. Have mom try to involve Lauren in another activity when Janet's friends come over.
7. Find an activity in which Lauren can join Janet and her friends.
8. Come up with a "code word" (e.g., strawberries) to signal that Janet needs some parental help with Lauren.
9. Reward Janet for handling situations without inappropriate behavior for one week by allowing her to have a friend stay overnight.
10. Each time Janet handles these situations by talking disrespectfully to Lauren or pushing her, her bedtime will be thirty minutes earlier.

---

Could you come up with any of your own? There are several other possible solutions to this problem as well as variations to the solutions already listed. Try to come up with two more.

### EVALUATE THE SOLUTIONS

This chart will help you organize your evaluation of suggested solutions. List the solutions in the left column and write the names of all participating "raters" above the remaining columns. In this case, both Janet and her parents gave ratings. Take a minute to review them.

| Solution | Janet | Mom | Dad |
|---|---|---|---|
| Push Lauren away | − | − | − |
| Tell Lauren you would like to play alone—repeat if necessary | + | + | + |
| Call Lauren a mean name | − | − | − |
| Go to your room to play | − | + | + |
| Mom and dad tell Lauren that Janet can play alone sometimes | + | + | + |
| Mom involves Lauren in another activity when Janet's friends visit | + | + | + |
| Find something that Lauren can do with Janet and friends | + | + | + |
| Use code word for Janet to get parental help | + | + | + |
| Reward Janet for responding well for one week | + | + | + |
| Thirty minutes of early bed for each time Janet acts inappropriately | − | + | + |
| _____ | ☐ | ☐ | ☐ |
| _____ | ☐ | ☐ | ☐ |
| _____ | ☐ | ☐ | ☐ |
| _____ | ☐ | ☐ | ☐ |

Enter your own solutions for this problem and rate them. Janet's parents allowed her to rate the solutions differently than they did, but they asked her to explain the reasons for several of her "+" and "-" evaluations and gave short explanations for why they rated the solutions as they did. This gave them the chance to have a good discussion with Janet and to learn more about how she views things.

### Pick a Solution

The first thing Janet and her parents did was to throw out any solutions they all had rated negatively and to focus on those that all had rated positively. This left eight possible solutions for them to consider, including two solutions that had only received one negative rating. After talking about these solutions in detail and thinking about how they might be combined, they devised the following plan:

1. Mom and dad will instruct Lauren that it is okay for Janet to have times when she plays alone or with her friends.
2. When possible, mom will try to involve Lauren in another activity when Janet wants to play alone with her friends.
3. Sometimes Janet will need to find a way to include Lauren in her activities, even if for a short time.
4. When she wants to play alone, Janet can say, "Lauren, I really want to play alone right now. We can play together later."
5. If #4 doesn't work, Janet can repeat it more firmly (but still respectfully).
6. If this does not help, Janet can move somewhere else or use the code word to get parental help.
7. If Janet does well for one week, she can have a friend stay overnight.
8. Each time Janet responds to Lauren with disrespectful talking or aggression (e.g., hitting, pushing), she will go to bed thirty minutes earlier.

If you look closely at this plan, you will see that the first two steps are ways to prevent the problem, the next four are replacement steps for Janet to take, and the following two are consequences that she will experience depending on how she chooses to respond to the situation.

### See If It Worked

Janet and her parents decided to talk together after one week to see how their plan was working. If it was working well, they would continue with it. If any of them felt that it needed to be improved, they would think together about how to do that by looking at their list of solutions and/or thinking of new ones.

The Detour Method and Problem-Solving Steps are two wonderful ways of teaching your children what you want them to do *instead* of problem behaviors. You should be able to use one of these two methods for almost any problem behavior. Sometimes you can use them both by using your Problem-Solving Steps to come up with a plan and then using the Detour Method to help your child learn the plan. Please take the time now to complete this section of your Parenting Plan by deciding which method for teaching positive behaviors will work best with your children and writing it (or both of them) down. Now that you know how to teach your children what you want them to do, let's take a look at how to effectively strengthen those new positive behaviors when they happen!

*five*

# Make Them Glad They Did It

## *How to Strengthen Positive Behavior*

Surely you will reward each person
according to what he has done.
Psalm 62:12

We have now come to third base, where we strengthen our children's positive behavior with rewards that teach them that positive behavior brings positive results. Two types of rewards will help us do that:

*social rewards:* a hug, a smile, parental attention, verbal appreciation for a desired behavior, a compliment, a pat on the back

*tangible rewards:* a special dinner, a favorite toy, an extension of a privilege, a trip to the park, a reasonable allowance

## Do Rewards Matter?

You have both given and been influenced by social and tangible rewards thousands of times before ever reading this book. They are a part of life. A smile, a touch, a comforting or humorous word, special attention, dessert following dinner, a grade on a report card, an allowance, a paycheck, a promotion—the list could go on—*all* function as rewards and influence the behavior and choices of those who receive them. For example:

> Laura is talking to Sam. If Sam looks at Laura, nods his head attentively, and responds in a way that lets Laura know that he was listening, how do you think Laura will feel? Laura will leave the conversation feeling glad that she talked with Sam. Why? Because Sam responded to Laura in a way that was positive, or *rewarding*, to her! If Sam keeps it up, Laura will learn that Sam is a good person to talk to and she will seek him out in the future. The point? Consistently rewarded behavior tends to happen more often.
>
> Julie is talking to Randy. Randy does not look at Julie, does not nod attentively, and responds to a question in a way that lets Julie know he has been dozing off. How do you think Julie will feel after their discussion? Lousy. Why? Because she has just been ignored for the last five minutes. Do you think that this will make Julie more likely to run to Randy the next time she wants to discuss something? Definitely not. Julie's conversation with Randy was *not rewarding* to her and if Randy keeps

*Consistently rewarded behavior tends to happen more frequently.*

it up, Julie will eventually find someone else to talk to. The point? Behavior that isn't rewarded tends to happen less often.

## God's Design

The fact that different types of rewards influence our choices is not a bad thing at all. God rewards our appropriate behavior and makes his intent to do so very clear. Scripture clearly promotes the idea of positive results, or rewards, following positive behaviors. Look, for example, at the following:

> If your enemy is hungry, give him food to eat;
>     if he is thirsty, give him water to drink.
> In doing this, you will heap burning coals on his head,
>     and the LORD will reward you.
>
> Proverbs 25:21–22

> I the LORD search the heart
>     and examine the mind,
> to reward a man according to his conduct,
>     according to what his deeds deserve.
>
> Jeremiah 17:10

> But when you pray, go into your room, close the door and pray to your Father, who is unseen. Then your Father, who sees what is done in secret, will reward you.
>
> Matthew 6:6

> For the Son of Man is going to come in his Father's glory with his angels, and then he will reward each person according to what he has done.
>
> Matthew 16:27

> . . . the Lord will reward everyone for whatever good he does, whether he is slave or free.
>
> Ephesians 6:8

As you can see, the concept of rewards following positive behaviors did not start with B. F. Skinner! God designed us so that we tend to do things that we view as being rewarding and to avoid things that we do not consider rewarding. This principle is true for our kids as well. Childhood behaviors, therefore, that are consistently rewarded tend to happen more frequently while behaviors that are not consistently rewarded or are followed by negative consequences tend to happen less often. As responsible parents we must use this principle effectively and purposefully to appropriately train our children.

Once you have taught your child what to do, you must consistently reward that behavior when it happens. You want your child to come to the conclusion that this behavior is worth doing. There are five ways of using rewards to strengthen positive behavior: social rewards, the Pour It On Technique, natural rewards, simple contracts, and negative reinforcement. Each of these tools will help you increase the frequency of your child's appropriate behavior, thereby reducing the amount of negative behavior left behind.[1]

## Social Rewards

Social rewards occur all the time. You have used them hundreds of times yourself. They are really just different ways of giving your child parental attention, which is *extremely* rewarding. Three primary types of social rewards will help you teach your child to behave more positively.[2]

### Specific Verbal Rewards

A specific verbal reward places a package of warm, parental attention at your child's doorstep and lets your child know *exactly* how to reorder any time he or she wants

to. The effectiveness of a specific verbal reward lies in letting your child know specifically what he or she did to earn
this reward, giving the reward immediately after the behavior, and doing this *consistently*.

Situation: Jenny is playing a game quietly, as opposed to
the loud and obnoxious manner in which she usually
plays a game.

Incorrect response: "Hey, look everybody, Jenny isn't driving everyone crazy!"

Correct response: "Jenny, I sure like it when you have a
quiet voice while we play a game." (This is stated immediately after the desired behavior is observed.)

Situation: You noticed that Peter just offered one of his
toys to his younger brother instead of keeping it to
himself.

Incorrect response: Say nothing or say, "It's about time
you started sharing."

Correct response: "Peter, I sure like it when you share
your toys with Jason. Good for you, you're learning
how to do it!" (Again, this is stated immediately after
the desired behavior is observed.)

Do you see how the positive behavior was *specifically*
identified? As I mentioned, parental attention is very rewarding to children. How would you feel if you were
Jenny or Peter and had just received that specific verbal
reward? You would feel great! A specific verbal reward
gives a child this type of parental attention and lets him
or her know *exactly* how to get it again—by doing the desired behavior. What more could you ask? This is an extremely effective tool that almost all of us could use more
than we do.

# Specific Verbal Rewards

- Let your child know *specifically* what he or she did to earn this reward.
- Give the reward *immediately* after the positive behavior.
- Use your specific verbal rewards *consistently!*

### General Verbal Rewards

A general verbal reward is also very motivating for a child. Consider the following phrases:

Good job!
Way to go!
Hooray!
Incredible!
Great!
You did it!
That's my girl!
Excellent!

These are all examples of general verbal rewards. There's no huge mystery or secret here—just fun, encouraging parental attention. These rewards differ from specific verbal rewards in that they do not identify your child's specific behavior. These phrases, however, are not only appropriate for scoring a goal for the soccer team or hitting a home run. They should also be used when your child does what you ask, shares, controls his or her anger, plays quietly, talks in a nice voice, and so on.

### Physical Rewards

For most people, physical touch is rewarding. There are some exceptions, so don't assume this principle applies to absolutely everyone. Most children, however, find a pat on the back, a gentle squeeze on the shoulders, a reassuring hug, and various other forms of physical affection to be quite rewarding. So as you use other social rewards, throw these in as you feel it is appropriate. A nice expression of physical touch can really accent a rewarding situation.

*Social rewards are very powerful tools that directly affect your child's behavior.*

Specific verbal rewards, general verbal rewards, and physical touch are three simple tools you can use every day, in almost any situation, to help your child learn to behave appropriately. Don't be fooled by their simplicity, though. These are very powerful tools that directly affect your child's behavior! Remember, they must be given immediately after the desired behavior and used consistently. What would you say in the following situations?

Situation: Brian, who usually screams when asked to go to Time-Out, turns and goes on your first command.
Correct response: _____

_____

Situation: Sarah has played cooperatively with her sister for the last fifteen minutes.
Correct response: _____

_____

Situation: Jordan picks up his toys at your first request (to your amazement!).
Correct response: _____

_____

While there are many correct possibilities, here are a few examples:

Brian: "Brian, you went to Time-Out the first time. Good job."
Sarah: "Sarah, I sure do like the way that you are playing and sharing with Jessica" (with a little squeeze on the shoulder).
Jordan: "Hey, you picked up your toys the first time I asked you. I sure like it when you do that."

## The Pour It On Technique

The Pour It On Technique gives you a strategic way to start using your social rewards. I highly recommend this technique, not just for the effect it will have on your child's behavior but also because it will get you into the habit of using your newly learned social rewards. You want these social rewards to become as natural to you as walking. And given time, they will. As the name implies, you are going to pour on the social rewards when you see your child exhibit specific desired behavior. Your child's appropriate behavior is the cereal and the social rewards are the milk. So, pour it on!

---

## The Pour It On Technique

1. Identify the target behavior that you want to strengthen.
2. Watch very carefully for that behavior to occur.
3. Whenever you see your child act in this way, *immediately* give him or her a specific verbal reward, such as, "Tommy, I sure love it when you play quietly with your toys!"

---

When identifying a target behavior, "acting good" is not specific enough. Here are some examples of specific target behaviors:

playing quietly
sharing toys at home
expressing anger appropriately
talking respectfully
following instructions the first time
showing appropriate table manners
playing properly with toys
cleaning up his or her bedroom
showing sportsmanship
putting away toys

Once you have determined the target behavior and have begun to teach your child how to do it, then you watch. Think of an eagle soaring high above the mountains, scouring the landscape, looking for any little movement on the ground that could signal its next meal. With the same type of watchful anticipation, you are waiting to see even a flicker of the target behavior. And when you finally see it, you immediately pounce upon it with an exuberant social reward. You pour it on! Why? Because Johnny has just shown you that he is starting to make progress toward the target behavior! And he can't take a second step until he has taken his first step. So, make him glad that he has started to move at all!

> Your child's appropriate behavior is the cereal and the social rewards are the milk.

This will not only begin to have a positive effect on his behavior but will affect the way he thinks about himself. Johnny will be consistently hearing realistically positive things about himself and his behavior. Even though inappropriate behaviors will still occur and negative consequences will still be given, your child will now be receiving regular feedback about the behaviors that he does right! You'll be teaching your child that although he occasionally makes mistakes and poor choices (who doesn't?), there are many things about him and his behavior that are positive. On top of that, using the Pour It On Technique will help you become more aware of positive behaviors (which were probably going unnoticed!) and more efficient at rewarding them.

When you start using the Pour It On Technique, I recommend you use a record sheet (see figure 2). It will help you stick to your task and will give you feedback on how many times you provided social rewards. Write in the date and the specific target behavior. Whenever you give a social reward, place an "X" in one box. Set a goal of giving

Figure 2

## Pour It On Technique

Complete the following chart for any two of the next seven days, placing an "x" in one box for every time you give your child a social reward for an appropriate behavior that day.

Day:_____ Behavior:_____

☐☐☐☐☐☐☐☐☐☐☐☐☐☐☐☐☐☐

Day:_____ Behavior:_____

☐☐☐☐☐☐☐☐☐☐☐☐☐☐☐☐☐☐

ten or more social rewards in a day and see how you do. Using this sheet should help you get into the swing of the Pour It On Technique and will give you exact information on how many social rewards you are giving. Once the positive behavior has become well established, you can begin to provide social rewards less frequently. This helps to maintain the behavior that your child has learned to do. But when you're trying to build a behavior that doesn't happen very often, remember to *pour it on!*

If your child rarely performs the desired behavior, make sure that you have clearly identified the behavior and that you have taught this behavior to your child. If needed, review or make changes in the steps you've used to teach the behavior. Then pour on the rewards whenever your child *comes close* to doing the target behavior. For example, if putting toys away is the target behavior, don't wait until they are all put away to give a verbal reward to your child. Give one *immediately* after your child puts a single toy away, or even after he or she simply picks up a toy to put it away.

Find something that you can reward!

## Natural Rewards

Once you have begun to regularly use the Pour It On Technique to help you with your specific verbal rewards, you are ready to begin using natural rewards. Natural rewards are built-in rewarding activities that your child experiences on a regular basis. They include television, snacks, free time, computer time, special treats, riding on the cart at the grocery store, watching videos, playing with friends, listening to the stereo, going fun places, and so on. Almost any preferred or enjoyable activity functions as a natural reward. Sit down and make a list of natural rewards that apply to your child. You will be surprised at how many there are.

Many children, however, don't realize that natural rewards are the result of positive behavior. Instead, they have grown to take natural rewards for granted. They may consider watching television to be a right rather than a privilege to be earned. Given such a viewpoint, natural rewards don't strengthen positive behavior because no connection is made between the two. It is your responsibility to wisely use natural rewards to teach your child about the link between positive consequences and positive behavior.

> Natural rewards are built-in rewarding activities that your child experiences on a regular basis.

When your child respects others, talks nicely, shares, follows parental requests, gets homework done, and so on, positive things tend to happen as a result. He or she gets along better with others, makes more friends, has more time for playing, and has more fun in general. These are natural rewards of positive behavior! When your child is disrespectful, talks rudely, refuses to share, is noncompliant, argues, and procrastinates about homework, unpleasant things tend to happen. He or she doesn't get along with others so well, loses friends, gets into trouble, and misses out on fun privileges.

So how do you use natural rewards to increase your child's positive behavior?

*Make sure that natural rewards do not immediately follow* inappropriate *behavior.* Remember, positive behavior needs to result in positive consequences; negative behavior needs to result in negative consequences. For example, if your child refuses to do her homework and is allowed instead to

go outside and play or watch television, then a natural reward just followed the wrong behavior and the wrong lesson was just learned. The loss of a natural reward (e.g., free
time) would have been a much more appropriate consequence for this behavior. Natural rewards should follow
*only* appropriate behaviors.

*As often as possible, make sure that natural rewards follow ap-
propriate behavior.* For example, if your child enjoys riding on
the grocery cart and behaves appropriately during the first
part of your grocery store trip, then let him ride on the cart
for the second half and point out that he is getting to ride on
the cart *because* he has behaved appropriately. This is a natural reward. When your child finishes all of her homework,
*then* she can go outside and play or watch television. Another
natural reward. If your child does a really good job of listening, you can point this out with a specific verbal reward and
provide a special surprise snack for being such a good listener.
If your child eats his dinner, then he gets to have dessert. If
your child does a good job of picking up her toys in the afternoon, then she can watch a short favorite videotape before dinner. Finishing chores on Saturday morning means
that the rest of the day is open for playing with friends. All
of these are examples of natural rewards following appropriate behaviors—a simple yet very effective combination.

*Point out the connection between the natural rewards and
the positive behavior.* This is the key step. When your child
displays appropriate behavior and experiences the natural
rewards that follow, you must teach him or her to recognize the natural link between the behavior and the consequences. For example, if your child has listened well and
completed her homework, you can say something like,
"We've had a really good afternoon. You worked hard and
got your homework done and have really listened well
today. Now we have time to have a snack and play a game
together. Good job!" By saying this, you are helping your

child to recognize the connection between her positive behavior and the resulting natural rewards. Otherwise, your child may have incorrectly concluded that the snack was coming just because it was snack time. Identifying this connection will help strengthen the positive behavior as your child becomes aware of the relationship between positive behavior and natural rewards.

*Use natural rewards to work on specific behaviors.* Occasionally choose a specific behavior that you would like to see improved (e.g., listening the first time, playing cooperatively, siblings getting along, etc.) and tell your child that if he or she does a really good job on that behavior for a certain time period (e.g., this day, the next two days, this week), then he or she will get to do something special (e.g., getting to pick a movie to watch, going someplace fun for lunch, having a friend over to play, playing a fun game with mom or dad, or staying up a little later). This is not to be delivered as a bribe ("Hey, little kid, come here . . ."), because it isn't a bribe. Instead, it is a way of teaching your child that positive behavior can be fun.

You can also use natural rewards effectively by surprising your child with a reward for appropriate behavior that he or she was not expecting (e.g., "Because you guys have been listening so good today, let's all go and get an ice-cream cone!"). All you are doing is emphasizing the natural relationship between positive behavior and positive consequences. You are teaching your child in a very easy, day-to-day fashion that positive behavior is fun and results in a variety of natural rewards.

Along with social rewards, natural rewards will be a tool that you will use on a daily basis. The main requirement for effectively using these two types of rewards is that you must be watching for your child's positive behavior. When you see it, be ready to respond immediately with a social and/or natural reward, and point out the connection between the natural reward and the behavior. You will be making sure that positive behavior is consistently rewarded and that your child learns that positive behavior brings positive results.

## Simple Contracts

A simple contract differs from the use of natural rewards in that it takes the positive consequences for a specific behavior and makes them unmistakably obvious for a certain amount of time. A simple contract is a turbocharged, laser-focused use of natural rewards, so to speak. Eventually, negative consequences can also be incorporated into a simple contract but, as you already know, we want to start with the positives. I like to think of using simple contracts as being similar to jumping a dead car battery. It would be nice if the battery were not dead, but for whatever reason, it is. No matter how much you have pleaded with the car, it has not started and it does not appear that it will start without a little assistance. Of course, your goal is for the battery to *stay* charged on its own, so you don't have to jump it every time you turn off the engine. But you've got to get it going before it can begin to charge on its own.

> A simple contract is a turbo-charged, laser-focused use of natural rewards.

This is the primary purpose of a simple contract. The goal is to get a behavior that is not happening to begin to happen. The goal is not to keep your child on a contract until he or she is eighteen, although some contracts (e.g., allowances) can be quite

helpful for teenage problems as well. Once the target behavior has begun to happen, the simple contract can be
phased out. The simple contract does not replace social
and natural rewards. It works *with* these rewards. Many
times, if you use social and natural rewards in a consistent
way, you will not even need to use a simple contract. In
fact, I often tell parents that it is the consistent use of social and natural rewards that really is the glue of the whole
approach. Simple contracts will come and go, but social
and natural rewards are meant to stay! However, for some
stubborn behaviors, a simple contract can be an extremely
helpful tool.

### Steps for a Simple Contract

1. *Specify the behavior you want to increase.* Just as we pre-
viously discussed, the behavior must be specifically identified, so that you (or your baby-sitter) can easily observe the
behavior and know whether or not it has occurred. Also,
make sure that you begin with just one behavior, to help
everyone get the hang of it. You can add other behaviors
later if you want to.

2. *Explain the contract to your child.* When introducing
your child to the contract, you don't need to explain all of
the details. Just let her know that together you are going
to work at helping her improve in a certain area. Simply
tell her that you have noticed that she has had a difficult
time with the specific behavior during the past few months
and that you are going to "make a contract" to help her get
better at this. Then, let her know that when she keeps her
end of the contract by improving her behavior, she will be
able to do some really fun things and get some special privileges as a result.

3. *Develop a simple menu.* You will eventually be giving
your child tokens or chips whenever you observe the target behavior. I have known families who used stickers, mar-

bles, pogs, poker chips, and a variety of other things. It doesn't matter what you use, as long as it is simple, fun, and cannot be easily counterfeited (e.g., pennies). For older children (nine and above), simply using "points" that are tabulated can be effective. First, however, you must decide on the rewards for which your child will be shooting. Rewards can be either tangible or social. In this context, we are expanding our definition of social rewards to include any activity or privilege that has a social element to it. Therefore, having a friend over after school and playing a game with mom are both examples of social rewards. Tangible rewards are extensions of privileges, activities, things to eat or drink, or items that can be purchased. Here is an example of a simple menu:

> 5 chips = one color pencil with eraser
> 10 chips = stay up thirty minutes later
> 20 chips = fishing with dad
> 30 chips = one trip to McDonald's
> 50 chips = one trip to the zoo

When you create Sarah's menu, you want Sarah to be as involved in the process as possible. Tell her that you want her to be able to earn some fun things as the result of working hard on the behavior that she is trying to improve. Help her come up with anywhere from five to ten items and write them down, making each item worth a certain number of chips. Tell Sarah that she can "trade her chips in" for items whenever she wants within reason and without violating regular family rules.

4. *Explain how the chips are earned.* Explain to Sarah *exactly* what she must do to earn her chips. You may even get Sarah's input as to how the desired behavior should be defined. For example, what do you mean by "making her bed"? What exactly does "cleaning up her room" include? What

are the steps for "controlling her anger"? If you have pre-viously taught her this behavior, this should already be done for you. Make sure the desired behavior is realistic, achiev-able, and extremely clear to everyone.

Once you have clearly specified the behavior that you want to improve, you need to decide how many points will be given for that behavior and how often. Some behaviors are easy. If a clean room consists of: (1) a tidy bed, (2) no clothes on the floor, and (3) dirty clothes in the hamper, then one chip can be given for each component. Or, a chip can be given only if all three components are done. Room checks can take place a specified number of times each week (e.g., Monday, Wednesday, and Friday) at an agreed upon time (e.g., 7:00 P.M.). A total of nine points can be earned each week.

Other behaviors are more difficult to quantify with points. Controlling anger, for example, can be tricky. When your child goes an hour without displaying inappropriate anger, how do you know if her anger was controlled or if she simply wasn't provoked during that hour? One answer is to limit the hours during which the contract applies, such as from after school until bedtime. Then you simply give your child the benefit of the doubt and award a point for every hour in which there are no anger problems. Another approach is to use response/cost, which is described in the next chapter.

5. *Write things down.* You will need to write down the specifics of your simple contract. This is particularly help-ful with older kids. So, draft a contract and make sure that you specify and define the target behavior and the system of rewards you intend to use. Once you have written things down, then post the simple contract in a readily accessible place (e.g., refrigerator or family bulletin board) for easy reference.

## Simple Contract Checklist

✔ The behavior you want to increase (e.g., keeping your room clean)

✔ A definition of this behavior (e.g., clothes put away, books on the desk, dirty clothes in the hamper, bed made, desk neat)

✔ How many points will be awarded for this behavior (e.g., one point for each of the five steps)

✔ How often points will be given (e.g., points awarded at room checks Monday, Wednesday, and Friday immediately after dinner)

✔ Child and parent signatures (to make it official)

6. *Review and adjust as needed.* Follow the contract for one week. Then take a look at how it is going. Ask yourself the following questions:

Is my child earning points?
Does my child seem excited about the contract? (Have I made it fun?)
Am I asking too much too quickly?
Are the steps or specific expectations clear to everyone?
Am I giving plenty of verbal social rewards?
Am I being consistent?
Am I giving the points *immediately* after the desired behavior occurs?
Have I adequately taught my child how to do the desired behavior?
Do I need to use different rewards?

If there are problems, the questions above may lead you to the answer. Each of these items is very important and failure to do any of them could reduce the success of the simple contract. Many times, slight adjustments need to be made that you couldn't have predicted. Ask yourself these questions, make adjustments if needed, and continue with the contract.

7. *Eventually phase out the contract.* After the desired behavior has increased and become stable, you can begin to phase out the simple contract. You do this by explaining to Sarah that she is doing wonderfully at the behavior and has become much stronger. As a result, she no longer needs the contract to help her as much. One of two things can then happen. She can receive fewer points for the same amount of behavior or have to do the behavior longer for the same amount of points. Choose whichever option seems the easiest for the particular behavior on which you are working. For example, instead of three points for a clean room, two points are given for a clean room. Once your child is successful at this, you can together decide when to stop the contract.

### Contract Tips

The tips below should help you as you set up your simple contract. However, if you find that the simple contract is just not working and you cannot figure out why this is, or if you are not sure how to define a specific behavior, set up the points, or develop a menu, or if your child's behavior is becoming increasingly problematic, consult a child therapist who is familiar with the types of problems your child is experiencing.

Make sure you phrase the target behaviors *positively*. Remember, you are trying to *start* a new behavior.

Start with small, achievable goals that your child will be able to accomplish. You can slowly increase the demands of the simple contract as your child masters the initial target behavior. Remember, you are setting your child up for success!

Chips must be given *immediately* following the desired behavior. If you are giving chips for a clean room, then hand your child her chips immediately after the room check. Do not save them up and give them all at the end of the night. We want the rewards for appropriate behavior to follow the actual behaviors as closely as possible. This helps make the connection between your child's behavior and the resulting positive consequences stronger and makes the contract more effective!

Do not hesitate to give "bonus points" for excellent behavior or effort. For example, you could give a bonus point if your child does a "perfect" job of cleaning her room for three consecutive room checks.

Your child will need a place to keep all of those chips. A fun project is to make a "bank" for chip storage. You can use anything you like. An empty jar, small box, or pouch can make a good bank. Your child can also decorate and personalize the bank. This can even be a nice thing to do together.

Occasionally, it will be necessary to change the items on the menu. After a while your child may become bored with the menu items and you can revitalize the contract by adding items or making a new menu from scratch.

## Negative Reinforcement

Many parents with whom I have worked originally thought that negative reinforcement meant the same thing as punishment. Not true. The presence of the word "reinforcement" means that negative reinforcement results in a behavior happening *more often* instead of *less often*. Let me tell you how it works.

Take a look at the circle in figure 3. Johnny is in the circle and wants to get out. He would rather be playing outside. So, we can say that being in the circle is a negative experience for Johnny. However, the exit is at the top of the circle. If Johnny discovered that he

Figure 3

could leave the circle by simply walking through the circle at any point, he probably would not take the time to walk all

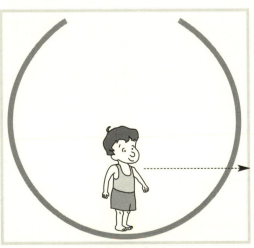

Figure 4

the way to the top of the circle to leave through the exit. Instead, he would walk out at a point in the circle much closer to him, as you see in figure 4.

The point is that when we are placed in a negative situation, we will often try to get out of that situation or to turn it off. And if Johnny learns that he can escape the circle simply by walking right through it, then guess what he will probably do the next time he is placed in the circle. That's right. He'll walk right through it again. Why? Because he has learned that walking through the circle works. The behavior that turns off the negative event will be more likely to happen the next time the negative event occurs. In other words, walking through the circle has been "negatively reinforced" because it got Johnny out of a negative situation.

There are many "negative situations," so to speak, that we place our kids in at one time or another. Telling them to do something, finishing homework, completing a chore, doing a Time-Out—these can all be unpleasant tasks from the child's point of view. Whenever a task like this is initiated (putting Johnny in the circle) the child may try to turn it off. If Johnny discovers that by arguing or whining he can escape having to do his homework or turn off the unpleasant task, then his arguing and whining have just been negatively reinforced. Why? Because they turned off the unpleasant experience of having to do his homework (just like Johnny walking *through* the circle). And you can bet that he will try them again the next time he doesn't want to do his homework!

There are many examples of how certain behaviors are negatively reinforced. Remember, whatever behavior *turns off* the negative event is reinforced. Examples of behaviors that are often accidentally negatively reinforced include screaming and shouting during a Time-Out, lying about homework assignments, arguing, whining, procrastinating, and ignoring parental requests. Any time your child can work his or her way out of a task or negative consequence by doing these things, these behaviors have just been reinforced.

Your task is simple. You have to make sure that the only behavior that turns off the negative event is a reasonable, desired behavior. Here are some examples of reasonable, desired behaviors:

| Situation | Reasonable Desired Behavior |
| --- | --- |
| Doing homework | Properly completing homework |
| Doing a chore | Finishing the chore within a reasonable time frame |
| Time-Out | Appropriately completing the Time-Out |
| Parental request | Following request or other appropriate response (e.g., asking a question, etc.) |

No other behavior should be successful at turning off the negative event. As you can see in figure 5, Johnny is discovering that he cannot walk right through the circle. Eventually, he will realize that the walls are no longer permeable and that if he wants to leave the circle, he must leave through the exit. In our example, the exit represents the reasonable,

Figure 5

desired behavior. The reasonable, desired behavior, then, is the only behavior that gets Johnny out of the circle and is the only behavior that gets reinforced. If this happens consistently, then Johnny will eventually learn that the exit is the only way out of the circle.

So, how do you use negative reinforcement with your child? Simple. When you place a demand on your child, you keep two things in mind:

You must have a clear idea of what you want your child to do (the reasonable, desired behavior).

You must make sure that this behavior is the *only* behavior that gets rewarded.

If completing the evening's homework is the demand, then the only thing that should "turn off" that demand is the reasonable completion of that homework. Any other "negative" response should not result in the cessation of that demand and could even result in a negative consequence. For example, if Johnny discovers that procrastinating or arguing about his homework *consistently* (there's that word again!) results in delaying the time at which he is allowed to play or watch TV, he will probably soon conclude that getting his homework done without arguing is the best solution. In this case, Johnny's parents made sure that the only behavior that got rewarded was completing his homework. Anything else produced a negative net result for Johnny.

If Sarah discovers that she can get out of having to comply with her mother's requests simply by whining about them for long enough, what behavior gets reinforced, or strengthened? That's right. Whining. However, if Sarah's mother makes sure that the only behavior that gets rewarded is timely compliance with her requests and that whining or any other inappropriate behaviors result in a

loss of parental attention, a Time-Out, or another negative consequence, Sarah is likely to eventually increase her
compliance to her mother's requests. Why? Because doing
anything else results in making her situation worse.

If you are thinking that increasing Sarah's compliance
could be made even easier by adding social rewards, the
Pour It On Technique, natural rewards, or even using a
simple contract, you are right! These tools can almost always be used together for best results.

## Pulling It All Together

We have just discussed how to reward positive behaviors through the use of social rewards, the Pour It On Technique, natural rewards, simple contracts, and negative reinforcement. These are all excellent tools and can be used
to increase the frequency of any positive behavior. But how
do you pull all of these ideas together? Here is a simple plan
that summarizes the ideas we have discussed thus far:

- Make sure that you are building a healthy relationship
  with your child.
- Consistently model appropriate parental behavior.
- Decide exactly what behavior you want your child to
  start doing.
- Make sure this behavior is specific and reasonable.
- Teach your child how to do the desired behavior, using
  either the Detour Method or Problem-Solving Steps.
- Consistently reward the desired behavior, using the
  Pour It On Technique and natural rewards.
- Make sure an inappropriate competing behavior is not
  being accidentally rewarded.
- Design a simple contract if needed.

We have now covered the first four essential ingredients of your Parenting Plan. Take the time to complete this section of your Parenting Plan by filling in specific ways that you can effectively strengthen your child's positive behaviors, using the tools in this chapter. Your plan is almost complete! Let's now move on to ways that you can begin to reduce the negative behaviors that are left over.

# six

# This Has Gotta Stop!

## *Bringing Negative Behavior to a Halt*

Discipline your son, and he will give you peace;
he will bring delight to your soul.

Proverbs 29:17

My personal and professional experiences have convinced me that most of us tend to immediately think about discipline when negative behavior arises in our children. We've spent the last four chapters, however, discovering that changing behavior isn't only about discipline. We must hit the ball and run around the three bases before we can reach home plate. Yet while relationship building, modeling, teaching, and positive reinforcement are extremely important tools for helping your child learn appropriate behaviors, discipline completes the process.

## Biblical Discipline

The Bible clearly admonishes parents to discipline children to help them learn to be godly and wise. Consider these passages:

> For these commands are a lamp,
> this teaching is a light,
> and the corrections of discipline
> are the way to life.
>
> Proverbs 6:23

> He who spares the rod hates his son,
> but he who loves him is careful to discipline him.
>
> Proverbs 13:24

> Discipline your son, for in that there is hope;
> do not be a willing party to his death.
>
> Proverbs 19:18

> Discipline your son, and he will give you peace;
> he will bring delight to your soul.
>
> Proverbs 29:17

> No discipline seems pleasant at the time, but painful. Later on, however, it produces a harvest of righteousness and peace for those who have been trained by it.
>
> Hebrews 12:11

These passages make one point very clear: As parents, we are responsible for appropriately and effectively disciplining our children. Just as God disciplines his children for their own good, so we are to discipline our children for their benefit. Corrective discipline should lead to life, hope, and wisdom. The Book of Proverbs describes the purpose of discipline as the attainment of wisdom. Discipline is a tool to help children become wise. True wisdom leads a person toward God, not away from him. The way you discipline your child should also have that effect.

The words used for discipline in Scripture teach us that in addition to merely providing chastisement for misbehavior, biblical discipline also provides instruction in godly and wise behavior (e.g., training for life, teaching how to make wise choices, warning of the consequences of foolish behavior). Biblical discipline teaches children how to live correctly and how to avoid the foolish traps of sin and poor decision making. It helps them to understand

> Discipline is a tool to help children become wise.

how appropriate behavior and wise decisions result in positive consequences and are an outgrowth of their relationship with God. There are two things you need to understand about discipline.

1. *We are commanded to discipline our children.* Scripture makes this very clear. By definition, biblical discipline is best understood as including instruction, training, and guidance, as well as correction. Sounds a lot like teaching, doesn't it?

2. *Discipline has a corrective, forward purpose.* Biblical discipline isn't punishment for punishment's sake. It is not a display of underdeveloped anger-control by a parent who is "getting even" with a child who has embarrassed him or her in public one too many times. It is not a lesson in, "I'll show you who's the boss around here." In fact, it is the opposite of all of those.

As parents we want children to learn to make wise decisions. Wise decisions about friends. Wise decisions about school. Wise decisions about listening to parents. Wise decisions about jobs. Wise decisions about relationships. Wise decisions about sex. Wise decisions about drugs. Wise decisions about God.

Discipline helps our children *learn* how to make wise decisions as they are growing up. We are not to discipline because we are angry (although we may be angry); we are to discipline because we want our children to learn from their behavior, even if the learning comes only in little steps. They need to learn that behaving appropriately and making wise choices pays off in a multitude of ways. It pleases God, results in more fun, enhances relationships, and helps avoid trouble. You also want them to learn that inappropriate behavior and poor decision making do not pay off and instead result in negative consequences that are not fun. You want to turn each *discipline* situation into the most effective *learning* situation that it can be.

> We want to turn each **discipline** situation into the most effective **learning** situation that it can be.

This is your goal when you discipline your children. If you do this as well as use all of your other teaching tools, you will be using discipline as it was meant to be used.

## Discipline Guidelines

We have established that discipline is one of the tools that we are to use to teach our children to make wise decisions. Following are a few general guidelines that will help you more effectively use discipline.

### Use Effective Commands

Prevention is one of the best cures for negative behavior. Some noncompliance can actually be the result of ineffective or unclear parental commands. Commands that are firm, clear, and respectful, on the other hand, can help get things going in the right direction from the start. Browse the following "command checklist" to see if your command style could use some brushing up:

1. *Make sure your child is listening.* When you give a parental command (e.g., "Johnny, please put your shoes away"), make sure that your child clearly hears you and understands what you want him to do. Make eye contact, minimize distractions (e.g., turn down the television), and occasionally have him repeat your command to make sure that he has fully understood.

2. *Speak clearly and firmly.* Make sure that your child knows the difference between your "play" voice and your "command" voice. I have heard parents give their children commands that left even me confused as to whether or not they were serious. Practice giving commands in a firm yet respectful tone of voice. If noncompliance is a real problem, make sure that you are not posing your commands as questions or favors; they are neither of these. You are really not *asking* Sally if she wants to go get her shoes; you are *telling* her to go get them.

3. *Don't speak in a threatening or militant tone.* While you are trying to give your commands in a firm manner, don't go overboard and become a drill sergeant. Barking out commands is appropriate for an officer but not for an effective parent. Billy isn't a new recruit; he's your son.

4. *Cut down on unnecessary commands.* Research has revealed that mothers of noncompliant children give far more commands to their children than mothers of compliant children. This makes sense. The more commands

there are, the more opportunities for noncompliance there are as well. So make sure that a command is important and necessary before you give it. This will make it easier for you to follow through consistently and easier for your child to keep from being overwhelmed with orders.

5. *Offer alternatives instead of just saying no.* For some of us, the word *no* can become a reflex response when a child asks a question. This contributes to behavior problems because your child is constantly being told what she *cannot* do instead of what she *can* do. Instead of letting your no be the last thing that echoes inside your child's mind following a request, reroute your child's energy in another direction by offering appropriate alternatives or by letting your child know when she *can* engage in that behavior (e.g., "Brittany, we don't have time to draw right now because we have to go out in a few minutes, but let's see if we can make time to draw tonight.").

### Do Not Lecture

Lecturing is typically ineffective and tiring for both you and your child. It also provides parental attention at exactly the wrong time if you give your lectures immediately after the misbehavior.

### Be as Matter-of-Fact as Possible

Keep your cool and redirect your child or give negative consequences in a simple, calm, and factual manner. This helps reduce emotional tension and keeps the interchange relatively short and to the point. This style of handling a discipline situation also places the emphasis on the child's behavior rather than on the child. Remember, you love your child; it is just certain behavior that you would like to improve.

### Use "Choosing" Language

As often as you can, slip the word *choose* (and its variations) into your dialogue with your child. For example, "Tommy, you can choose to listen or you can choose a Time-Out." (Tommy doesn't listen.) "Okay, Tommy, you chose not to listen so you just chose a Time-Out. Let's go." If you make this a regular habit, you will be teaching your child that *he* is responsible for his behavior. You will be helping him to learn that he is constantly making decisions and that the ability to make wise ones is always within his grasp.

### Make Sure the Reason for Discipline Is Clear

You want to make every discipline situation a *learning* situation. To do this, you must help your child see the connection between her inappropriate behavior and the resulting consequence. You don't want Cindy to think that she was placed in Time-Out just because you were angry. You want her to understand that the Time-Out was the result of her *choice* to continue misbehaving.

### Teach Your Child How to Avoid the Consequences

Remember, you are trying to teach and encourage your child to make the *right* decisions! Make all of the options clear, along with the positive and negative consequences that go with each.

### Encourage Better Choices in the Future

This can come in handy when your child develops the "How can you do this to me?" syndrome. Sometimes, negative consequences really seem like a fate worse than death to a child. Johnny can have a hard time seeing past the temporary inconvenience of the negative consequence. If

your child starts arguing or complaining about the consequence, do two things.

First, remind your child that the same situation does not
have to happen tomorrow. Make it clear that he is still
going to bed early tonight, but tomorrow night he doesn't
have to. Tomorrow he can stay up until his regular bedtime
as long as he behaves appropriately. Tomorrow can be a
better day! It is all up to your child. Regularly reminding
him of this will help him learn to look past the current situation and keep the negative consequence in perspective.

Second, if your child continues to argue after you have
reminded him of this, just leave. Standing around listening to him argue only teaches him that arguing gets your
attention. Instead, Johnny needs to learn that arguing gets
him absolutely nothing, except possibly more negative consequences if it becomes excessive.

### Discuss Behaviors from a Biblical
### and Relational Perspective

During positive times or after negative consequences
have been completed, you can make the most out of your
child's misbehavior by occasionally discussing the behavior with your child, examining the effects of that behavior
upon relationships (e.g., with friends, siblings, parents,
etc.), reviewing the consequences that tend to follow that
behavior, or looking at the behavior from a biblical perspective. Make sure that these discussions are relatively
short, and do not give in to the temptation to turn them
into a lecture. Remember, longer is not better!

Try discussing the behavior in the third person to take
the spotlight off of your child (e.g., "If a girl got mad and
decided to hit someone, how would the person she hit feel?"
and "What does God say about that?"). Make sure that your
child knows that her behavior is forgiven and that you do
not expect perfection from her. Sharing some of your own

struggles and successes with that behavior in a very simple way can add a nice touch. Allow your child to do as much of the talking as possible and end the discussion on a positive and encouraging note.

### Practice Positive Behavior

As we have discussed, biblical discipline includes more than just negative consequences for misbehavior. You need to make sure that your child knows how to do the positive behavior that can replace the inappropriate behavior. Using the Detour Method or Problem-Solving Steps, talk about which behaviors would be more appropriate the next time the situation arises. For more ideas on how to do this, review chapter 4.

### Be Consistent

We all walk through doors instead of trying to walk through walls because we have learned that trying to walk through walls *never* works. The walls are consistently there. The application to family life is that misbehavior must be addressed consistently if you want your children to learn the rules. If misbehavior received negative consequences yesterday, is overlooked today, and will be accidentally rewarded tomorrow, your child is learning that two out of three times, the behavior seems to pay off! What your child needs to learn is that misbehavior virtually never pays off. This is only learned through consistency. Your goal is to make sure that nega-

> *Biblical discipline includes more than just negative consequences for misbehavior.*

tive behaviors are consistently followed by an appropriate negative consequence. No one is perfect at this, but if you put your mind to it you can be consistent most of the time.

## Behavior Weakening Tools

We will discuss five behavior weakening tools in this chapter: Time-Out, natural consequences, logical consequences, ignoring, and response/cost.[1] I call them "behavior weakening" tools because that is exactly what they are designed to do: weaken inappropriate behaviors. Each of these tools is extremely effective when used correctly alongside efforts to teach and strengthen positive behaviors, build relationships, model appropriate behavior, and improve family communication. Remember, your overall plan is to teach your child what to do and then effectively strengthen that behavior. Then, as needed, you can weaken the inappropriate behavior at the same time. Discipline tools always work better when used in a positive environment.

> Discipline tools always work better when used in a positive environment.

### Time-Out

If used correctly, Time-Out can be a very helpful behavior weakening tool for children ages two to twelve. To use it correctly, however, you must first understand what it is and how to make it work for you.

The name Time-Out is actually a short version of the longer title, Time-Out from Positive Reinforcement. The effectiveness of Time-Out lies in the fact that *all* sources of positive reinforcement are *removed* from your child for a set period of time following misbehavior. Negative behavior turns off a positive. This is not fun for a child. The emphasis, of course, is placed on your child's choice and the consequences that accompany that choice.

How do you remove all possible sources of positive reinforcement? The key is picking a good Time-Out spot. This is where most mistakes happen. Many parents tell me that they have their children do Time-Out on the living-room couch, at the kitchen table, or in the child's bedroom. While sending a child to his room or having him sit in a dining-room chair for a few minutes can be a very helpful thing to do in order to give him some time to cool off or to reconsider a situation, it is not what I consider the best spot for a Time-Out. Just think of all the positive things children can hear, see, and do in these settings. They can hear the radio, watch the television, look out the window, see the frustrated look on your face, do little things to get your attention, play with toys, read a book, look at posters, and so on. Each of these things can be rewarding or entertaining to a child and will zap the effectiveness out of a Time-Out! Think about the lesson being taught to your child: I do something wrong and I get to sit on the couch for a while, or go to my room and read. Not a bad deal. Not a good Time-Out.

For a Time-Out spot to be maximally effective, there is one word you must consider: boring. An effective Time-Out spot has to be as devoid of positive reinforcement as is humanly possible. Consequently, the best Time-Out spots are the most boring places on the face of the earth. Or at least the most boring places in your house. How do you find a good Time-Out spot? All you have to do is to pick a possible Time-Out spot and then go and sit there for a few minutes. What do you hear? What do you see? What can you do? How boring would it be for you to sit there for several minutes? If you start thinking that this exercise isn't any fun, you have probably found a good Time-Out spot. Every house is different and you will have to decide where the best Time-Out spot is for you. Effective Time-Out spots may include the bathroom, laundry room, a spare room, or a boring corner or hallway spot. You want your Time-Out spot to be as boring as possible while still being safe for your child and providing you with the ability to monitor behavior as necessary.

So how can you put Time-Out to work for you? Let's look at six steps:

1. *Select the behavior you wish to decrease and describe it in clear and specific terms.* For example, inappropriate expression of anger (e.g., hitting, kicking, name-calling) could be a "Time-Out behavior."

2. *Select your Time-Out spot.* Pick the most boring place you can find. Try it for a while and see how it works. If it doesn't seem to be weakening the negative behavior, then perhaps you need a different spot. Once you have found a truly boring spot, stick with it. Remember, boring is the key.

3. *Inform your child that you will be using Time-Out.* Explain exactly how a Time-Out can be earned, being sure you have also taught your child how a Time-Out can be avoided. Walk through the entire procedure a few times, using the following sample instructions as a guide:

Johnny, you know that sometimes when you *(state the problem behavior)*, Mom and Dad get angry and you often get into trouble. Well, we are going to start something new at home to help you get better at *(state the de-*

*sired behavior)* so that everyone will be happier. We are going to do something called a Time-Out. A time-out is what coaches call in basketball games to stop the clock so they have time to think and get their team back in control. We are going to use it at home too. Here is how it will work.

From now on, when you *(state the problem behavior)*, you can make a choice. You can choose to stop doing it, or you can choose to go to Time-Out. If you choose to stop doing it, that will be great! If you choose a Time-Out, you will go to *(selected spot)* and you will sit there for three minutes. I will set this timer so you will know when Time-Out is over. It will be right over here. You can use this time just like coaches do in basketball games; to calm down and get back in control. If you have been under control for those three minutes, which means calmly sitting in your chair, you can come out of Time-Out and everything will be okay. If you do not get yourself under control (e.g., if you shout, hit the wall, leave the Time-Out spot), you will earn one extra minute *each time* I have to remind you to get yourself under control. Do you understand?[2]

4. *Walk your child through the Time-Out procedure.* I recommend sitting in the Time-Out spot yourself and modeling appropriate (e.g., sitting quietly, taking deep breaths, trying to calm yourself down) and inappropriate (e.g., shouting, stomping feet) Time-Out behavior. Then have your child do the same. If you think your child may have difficulty calming himself down, you can also teach him a few statements that he can quietly say to himself when in Time-Out, such as, "I need to be calm so I can get out of Time-Out," "I want to control my temper," and so on. When your child demonstrates appropriate Time-Out be-

havior during this rehearsal, make sure to follow this with specific verbal rewards. This is the behavior we want him to do when in Time-Out. Teach him how to do it right!

5. *When your child displays inappropriate behavior, offer the choice of improved behavior or a Time-Out.* Some behaviors, such as hitting, may automatically result in a Time-Out. Do not debate, lecture, or argue with your child once he has chosen a Time-Out. This can actually be reinforcing to him. Instead, be as matter-of-fact as possible and with as little parental attention as you can give, take him immediately to Time-Out. It should go something like this:

> (Johnny takes a toy from his brother.) "Johnny, you need to share your toys with your brother or you will choose a Time-Out." (Johnny grabs another toy from his brother.) "Okay, Johnny, you have just chosen to go to Time-Out. Let's go."

6. *Use a kitchen timer to keep track of the Time-Out period.* I recommend starting with three minutes of Time-Out. Then add one extra minute to the timer every time your child displays inappropriate Time-Out behavior. In a matter-of-fact way, tell your child that you have observed the inappropriate behavior and he has earned an extra minute of Time-Out, and remind him of the appropriate behavior that he needs to do while in Time-Out. This approach places the choice of how long the Time-Out will be entirely with your child. Appropriate Time-Out behavior results in a Time-Out that lasts only three minutes. Inappropriate Time-Out behavior results in a Time-Out that can last up to about thirty minutes.

Hint: If you use a room for Time-Out, such as the bathroom, place the timer right outside the door so your child can hear it but not play with it. Keep the door ajar by about twelve inches so that the door is mostly closed but so that you can hear what your child is doing and stick your head in to monitor his behavior at any time.

Once you learn to give Time-Out correctly, it can be one of your most effective behavior weakening tools. However, it is not always easy to do and sometimes children can pose challenges to Time-Out. Here are some tips for those challenging situations:

### Your Child Refuses Time-Out

Say that you want her on her way by the time you count to three. If your child continues to refuse, provide minimal physical assistance (i.e., guiding by the arm or shoulder), making sure not to debate, argue, or provide attention.

If this doesn't work, don't battle with your child or get into a wrestling match. Firmly inform your child that she will be choosing the loss of a privilege (e.g., TV, books, toys, visiting friends) for the rest of the day if she does not go to Time-Out immediately. If your child wants to discuss the situation, tell her that you will be happy to discuss it after she completes the Time-Out. If your child chooses the loss of privileges by continued refusal to go to Time-Out, inform her of this in a matter-of-fact manner and walk away.

In a situation like this, refusing to go to Time-Out must be followed by a negative consequence that your child will experience as being *worse* than the Time-Out. Remember our discussion about negative reinforcement? It applies here. If the alternative negative consequence is *better* than the Time-Out from your child's perspective, then she will continue to resist going to Time-Out. While you want to make sure that the loss of privilege is not extreme or unfair, it should be unpleasant enough to encourage your child to go to Time-Out next time. See the section on logical consequences if you need help with ideas.

## Your Child Misbehaves While in Time-Out

It is likely that your child is testing you. In essence, he may be saying, "I am not going to sit here in Time-Out. Watch me!" Your child may also have a difficult time controlling his temper. Either way, your goal is to help your child calm himself down and complete the Time-Out. If you suspect that this will be difficult for your child, then make sure to teach your child one or two relaxing techniques, such as taking deep breaths or counting backward from ten, when you originally introduce the Time-Out procedure. Remember, teaching him what *to do* when in Time-Out will give him a better chance of succeeding when he actually does his Time-Out.

If your child is misbehaving during a Time-Out, firmly remind him of the rules for Time-Out (e.g., "To get out you must sit quietly and calmly until the bell dings"). Also remind him that out-of-control behavior will earn him extra minutes, and add minutes to the timer as necessary. If your child continues to misbehave, be sure to do the following:

1. *Complete the Time-Out.* If you discontinue the Time-Out due to your child's tantrum, you will have rewarded him for misbehaving. For Time-Out to be successful, the only behavior that should bring a Time-Out to an end is appropriate "Time-Out behavior." Anything else should result in more time or additional negative consequences. If your child breaks anything while in Time-Out, he should have to replace it. If your child becomes extremely disruptive, destroys property, or poses any threat of harm to himself or others, consult a qualified child therapist immediately.

2. *Allow appropriate expression of anger.* Remember, children are not usually at their best when they have just earned a Time-Out. As such, it is inappropriate to expect them to sit there like a statue when they are angry and upset. If your

child has a hard time with his temper, it may be a victory simply to get him to remain in Time-Out. Make sure that you have taught him what to do when in Time-Out (e.g., take deep breaths, remind himself to calm down, focus on successfully completing the Time-Out) and then encourage him to do this during the Time-Out. For some children, it can help to tape a list of calming Time-Out thoughts and behaviors to the wall in the Time-Out area to help remind them how to calm down and get back in control.

Use your own judgment about what type of anger expression to allow while in Time-Out. The goal and general guideline is to have your child calm himself down in a *relatively quiet manner*. In most cases, you should stick to these guidelines and add additional minutes when they are broken. However, for children who have a harder time with anger-control, a mild shout or two may be worth ignoring *in the beginning* if it means that your child will complete the rest of the Time-Out. Then, once your child gets used to completing his Time-Outs, you can begin to work more specifically on improving his anger expression while in Time-Out.

3. *Give specific, verbal rewards for successful Time-Out completion.* Your goal is to teach your child to successfully complete his Time-Outs. When your child completes a good Time-Out, let him know that he has done a good job. Say something like, "Johnny, you did a good job sitting calmly in Time-Out just now. Good for you." Remember, behaviors that are consistently rewarded tend to happen more often.

### TIME-OUT LASTS TOO LONG

A Time-Out should not last more than twenty or thirty minutes. If your child's Time-Out goes this long, your child has probably made it a personal goal not to go along with the Time-Out. You must remain in control of the situation.

Here's what you do. Enter the Time-Out area and firmly inform your child that Time-Out is now over (this is your decision, not hers!) and that by choosing not to behave appropriately in Time-Out, she has now *chosen* the loss of a privilege for the rest of the day. Stay calm and deliver this message in a matter-of-fact way. If you suspect that your child may push Time-Out to its time limit, make sure that you have thought this situation through beforehand and are already prepared with a negative consequence to deliver. *The more prepared you are, the calmer you will be.* This is not the time for coming up with negative consequences off the top of your head.

The net result for your child will be having spent half an hour in Time-Out and losing a privilege for the rest of the day. Regardless of how good your child is at math, she will soon realize that this is far worse than simply completing her initial three minutes of Time-Out.

### You Are Away from Home

When you are away from home you have two options: do Time-Out right where you are or use a Time-Out ticket. When possible, doing a Time-Out right where you are is always preferable. If you are at a friend's house, ask if there is a good Time-Out spot that you can use. When at a public place, you might be able to have your younger child sit facing a wall for a Time-Out if you can find a good spot.

However, due to the problems with finding an effective Time-Out spot away from home, a Time-Out ticket can be a helpful alternative. Go to your local party supply store and buy some tickets like those you would get at a movie theater. These will be your Time-Out tickets. When your child misbehaves in public, warn him that further inappropriate behavior will earn a Time-Out as soon as he gets home. If the inappropriate behavior continues, give your child a Time-Out ticket and inform him that he will serve a Time-Out immediately upon returning home. The use of a ticket helps make the consequence more immediate. Then make sure you follow through!

### Natural Consequences

Natural consequences allow your child to experience the natural results of her behavior. You simply and calmly "step out of the way" and let the consequences do the work. Of course, you *never* utilize natural consequences when the consequences could injure or otherwise harm your child. In other words, you don't teach your child how to cross the street by letting her get hit by a car! Here are some examples of natural consequences:

| Behavior | Natural Consequence |
|---|---|
| Sally refuses to eat | She misses that meal and gets hungry |
| Sally intentionally breaks a toy | She does not get the toy replaced |
| Sally refuses to get up in the morning | She is taken to school "as is" |

As you can see, natural consequences bring a child face-to-face with reality. This is why they can be so effective. Many parents, however, find it difficult to allow the natural consequence to take place. Different parents have different "comfort levels" with natural consequences. One mother took her daughter to school in pajamas one morning because she was never ready on time (after that, she got ready on time!), but other parents may not feel comfortable with that scenario. It will be up to you to find your level of comfort with natural consequences. Once you find it, using an appropri-

> Simply and calmly "step out of the way" and let the consequences do the work.

ate natural consequence can be a *great* learning experience for your child.

### Logical Consequences

Natural consequences are not always available in every situation. However, you can almost always think of a logical consequence that will be appropriate for a misbehavior. The beauty of logical consequences is that they allow your child to experience consequences that are logically related to his misbehavior. This logical connection between your child's behavior and the negative consequence helps make the experience a great teaching tool. Logical consequences, like natural consequences, teach invaluable lessons that are based in reality. They provide children with the types of consequences that real life tends to bring. This helps your child to become aware of the social, behavioral, and interpersonal effects of his choices. Logical consequences prove useful with both children and adolescents. In fact, logical consequences are the discipline tool of choice for teenagers. So you might as well get skilled at giving them now. Here are some examples of logical consequences:

| Behavior | Logical Consequence |
|---|---|
| Tommy neglects his homework | He loses free time privileges until his homework is done or has to do his homework *before* school in the morning |
| Tommy damages property | He must pay for repair or do work around the house to pay for the damages |
| Tommy throws a tantrum | He chooses a Time-Out |
| Tommy neglects his chores | He loses privileges that are dependent on chore completion |
| Tommy breaks his curfew | He must come home earlier the next evening |
| Tommy makes a big mess | He must clean it up before doing fun activities |
| Tommy colors on the wall | He must clean the wall |
| Tommy never gets up on time | He goes to bed earlier until the problem is solved |

| Tommy talks rudely to his parents | He loses fifteen minutes of a special privilege (e.g., Nintendo time, TV time) or a percent of his allowance for each incident |

You can see how logical consequences can be applied to a wide variety of situations. Your job is to simply and creatively devise consequences for misbehavior that "fit the crime." There are few things in the world of negative consequences more beautiful than a nicely devised logical consequence! Once you get used to it, coming up with logical consequences will become relatively easy. Sometimes, however, you have to be creative. Having a child finish uncompleted homework in the morning before school is an example of a creative logical consequence. Occasionally, you will simply have to resort to linking a desired activity

*Logical consequences teach invaluable lessons that are based in reality.*

(e.g., free time, computer games, TV, etc.) to a certain negative behavior. However, you can still make this logical by simply explaining to your child that special privileges are logically related to certain reasonable behaviors (e.g., showing respect to others, doing homework, etc.). It's a package deal.

### Ignoring

Because parental attention is extremely rewarding, behaviors that are consistently followed by immediate parental attention will tend to be strengthened regardless of whether that behavior is positive or negative. If a negative behavior is being rewarded by parental attention, the immediate removal of attention following that behavior can sometimes help the behavior to be weakened.

This is sort of the reverse of the Pour It On Technique. With that technique, we chose desired behaviors and systematically set out to reward them with various forms of parental attention. Here, we are trying to make sure parental attention does *not* follow certain undesired behaviors. Of course, this tool is only useful if you think that your attention is helping to sustain the inappropriate behavior. If the behavior is being rewarded in other ways, then removing your attention may have little, if any, effect. Also, behaviors that are aggressive, destructive, or potentially harmful should not be ignored because of the damage they inflict. Other responses will be more appropriate in those cases.

A classic example of an appropriate situation for this technique is the two-year-old's temper tantrum. The average two-year-old's tantrum results when a child feels frustrated and upset about not getting something she wants and not having the verbal or problem-solving skills to more effectively handle the situation. Responding to the tantrum with attention or by giving in to the child teaches her that throwing a tantrum can be a very effective way to get what she wants. However, if you ignore the tantrum by looking away or even walking away, thereby removing all parental attention from your child, the lesson she learns is that throwing tantrums does not get her what she wants but rather results in a loss of parental attention until she again begins to display appropriate behavior.

As you face inappropriate behaviors from your child, evaluate the possibility of using this method by carefully identifying mild to moderate inappropriate child behaviors that do not result in harm to anyone or destruction of property. Then determine if you have been reinforcing these behaviors with parental attention. If so, begin to con-sistently withdraw attention (verbal, eye contact, body po-sition) immediately after the onset of these behaviors. If not, try another approach.

### Response/Cost

Response/cost is a very effective way of specifically con-necting inappropriate behaviors with consequences. This form of discipline can be used for both home and school behaviors. When using response/cost, the parent gives the child something of value (e.g., six chips, one hour of video game time divided into ten-minute segments) at the be-ginning of the day. Then, whenever the child performs an undesired behavior, such as a tantrum, hitting, or receiv-ing poor marks on a school behavior chart, he loses one of the desired objects (e.g., one chip, ten minutes of video game time). Each undesired response costs the child some-thing positive. As many chips or points as are left at the end of the day, or by a specified time, belong to the child. Points or chips can be tied into a simple contract and menu (see chapter 5) or regular household privileges that have been divided into time segments (e.g., TV, video games, outside playtime) can be used. A response/cost program could work as follows:

> Johnny is a ten-year-old boy who throws tantrums (e.g., shouts, throws things, kicks wall) when he is angry. His tantrums occur primarily after school, between 3:00 and 9:00 p.m. To use a response/cost approach, his mother gives him five chips each day after school. Each time Johnny exhibits the specified tantrum behaviors he loses one chip. This means that Johnny's mother literally goes to his room and removes one of the chips that she had placed in his "chip bank." If Johnny's mother was using

tabulated points instead of chips, she would verbally inform him that he had lost a point and then add the remaining points to his total at the end of the day. Johnny can also earn bonus chips for consecutive days of no-tantrum behavior. He can use his chips to purchase items from a menu, just as he would with a simple contract.

As the tantrums become less frequent, Johnny's mother lets him know how wonderful he is doing at learning to control his temper. Then, she begins to phase out the response/cost program by telling Johnny that he does not need the chips to help him as much as he did before and that he can start with just four chips a day now. Eventually, she can move to three chips. Using bonus chips for excellent behavior (e.g., three days in a row with no tantrums) is a great way to help your child adapt to earning fewer chips overall. At some point, Johnny and his mother will decide to discontinue the response/cost program because Johnny has gotten so good at controlling his temper that he does not need it anymore and there are plenty of natural rewards for displaying good anger-control. Of course, the simple, verbal rewards will still be coming strong!

## What about Spanking?

Many loving parents have administered mild spankings on occasion and have produced children who have grown up to be healthy, well-adjusted adults. However, I have talked with a growing number of parents who prefer to use other discipline tools to teach their children appropriate behavior. To help you sort through the issues surrounding spanking, let's take a look at what the Bible has to say.

### Is Spanking Biblical?

Solomon clearly identifies the need for discipline to cultivate wisdom. He encourages both corrective discipline of misbehavior and prescriptive instruction of appropriate behavior. We must *teach* our children to be wise and godly, says Solomon: "Train a child in the way he should go, and when he is old he will not depart from it" (Prov. 22:6). This is the purpose of discipline—training, teaching, and wisdom.

Several times in the Book of Proverbs Solomon refers to using the "rod" in the discipline of children (e.g., Prov. 22:15; 23:13–14). We must, however, consider these verses within their historical and cultural context. For example, consider these verses as a reflection of the discipline practices of Solomon's time. Then we can see Solomon's attempt to teach wise parenting principles in terms consistent with cultural practices of his day.

> The Bible neither commands nor prohibits spanking.

As a whole the Bible balances Solomon's references to physical punishment with instructions for parents to display love, patience, understanding, and self-control, and to consistently model appropriate behavior. Consider Paul's exhortation to fathers: "Do not exasperate your children; instead, bring them up in the training and instruction of the Lord" (Eph. 6:4). Paul calls for a balanced parenting style focused on training and instructing children in godly behavior.

Suffice it to say, then, that Solomon's references to physical punishment as one form of discipline do not constitute a command to spank your children. Instead, he emphasizes the important role of discipline in raising children by using an example (i.e., discipline with a rod) that would be easily understood in his culture. Nowhere does he imply that you disobey God if you *do not* spank your children. The Bible neither commands nor prohibits spanking. It allows appropriate spanking as a discipline option, but doesn't necessarily promote it as a more biblical form of discipline than other approaches. Biblical parenting, therefore, is possible with or without spanking.[3]

### *Is Spanking Effective?*

An intelligent decision about spanking requires both identification of relevant biblical principles and evaluation of its effectiveness as a teaching tool. After all, teaching is what discipline is all about. Several relevant facts deserve our consideration at this point.

*Frustrated parents may resort to physical punishment simply because it is easy and offers an emotional release.* Not all spankings result from emotional parental overload, but frustration and the lack of a proactive plan can push a parent to use spanking rather than other effective approaches. For example, proactively working on teaching and reinforcing positive behavior, following through with a Time-Out, or thinking of a logical consequence takes time, energy, and planning. A spur-of-the-moment spanking does not. Frustration and the lack of a proactive plan often push parents to use spankings rather than other more effective approaches. My two sons frequently remind me that as well as being rewarding, parenting can be amazingly frustrating at times. I can remember many instances when I have wanted to spank one of them because I was *so* frustrated (kicking the back of the driver's seat in the car comes to mind!). I have occasionally given mild spankings in these situations. I would have been wiser, however, to cool off before making a discipline decision instead of spanking out of frustration. Spanking because you don't want to take the time to consider other alternatives is not a good reason to spank.

*Frequent physical punishment models aggression.* When you use spanking as a primary discipline tool, you repeatedly show your child how *you* address problems when you are angry. There is simply no way around it—spanking, like anything else, can be overused. Furthermore, you also miss out on wonderful opportunities to teach your child, by your example, how to solve problems and think of solutions in other effective ways.

*Physical punishment does not teach the social or "logical" consequences of inappropriate behavior.* Spanking teaches a child that if he exhibits a certain behavior, he will experience some physical pain. Where else in real life does this ever happen? Teachers don't spank you. Other children don't spank you. When you are a teen or an adult, people don't spank you. Physical punishment is not intended to be the primary method through which social behavior is taught. Relying heavily on spanking to address misbehavior robs your child of the opportunity to experience consequences more "logically" connected to behavior. Life is bursting at the seams with examples of natural and logical consequences. If you break something, you have to pay for it. If you annoy someone, you lose the opportunity to play with him or her. If you don't get your homework done, you don't get certain privileges. If your chores don't get done, your allowance is reduced. If you don't eat your dinner, you get hungry. These types of real-life consequences teach your children real-life lessons.

*There are many other effective approaches for addressing childhood misbehavior.* Occasional mild spanking used along with other behavior weakening tools for younger children cannot be directly linked to any negative outcomes. In fact, used within the context of healthy family relationships, occasional spanking can be one component of an effective approach to misbehavior. But can discipline be effective without spanking? Definitely. Research studies have shown that consistent use of positive reinforcement, Time-Out, and logical consequences effectively increase appropriate behavior and reduce misbehavior. I've seen this take place time and again, even with the hardest-to-handle child. When used consistently, these tools can be a lifesaver.

### Is Spanking Appropriate?

In certain situations a mild spanking can be an effective teaching tool. I recommend limiting an occasional spanking to children between the ages of two and six. Examples of when spanking may be useful include a young child engaging in a dangerous behavior (e.g., running toward the street, reaching to touch a hot stove) or situations requiring a back-up negative consequence (e.g., when a young child refuses to stay in a Time-Out chair). Even in these situations, however, there are other approaches that can also be effective.

I have two major concerns about spanking. I am concerned when parents spank their children either too harshly or too frequently. There are parents who have taken spanking dangerously close to the line that separates physical punishment from physical abuse. Unfortunately, there are too many parents who have crossed over that line and their children have paid a heavy price for their parents' lack of self-control. Other parents don't spank too harshly, but they rely on spanking as their primary discipline tool. This means that whenever their children misbehave in any way, some form of spanking almost certainly lies around the corner. That's a lot of spanking and a lot of missed opportunities in which a more effective form of discipline could have been used.

If you do choose to give your child a mild spanking, make sure it is given in a controlled and matter-of-fact manner and is not misperceived by your child as rejection or as a withdrawal of your love. At some point after the spanking, have your child explain to you the reason for the spanking and help your child identify steps to take in order to avoid the same type of misbehavior in the future. I define a mild spanking as two to four swats with an open hand, on the buttocks, over the clothes. It should be hard enough to cause mild to moderate discomfort but never hard enough to leave welts, bruises, or in any way injure a child. Spanking is allowable, physical abuse is not. That's why I discourage spanking with an object rather than using an open hand. An open hand provides a much more accurate barometer of how hard you are spanking your child, helping to ensure that you do not spank with inappropriate force. If you use a neutral object, you have no such barometer and are in danger of accidentally hitting your child harder than you may realize.

The decision about whether or not to spank is yours. Effective behavior change can be achieved with or without the appropriate use of spanking. If you do choose to occasionally use spanking, don't rely on it as your primary discipline tool. Instead, work on using other discipline tools and develop a proactive plan for effectively addressing problem behaviors. If you do, you will likely find that your child's behavior will improve even without spanking. A consistent combination of behavior strengthening and behavior weakening tools is the best package that you can get (along with relationship building, parental modeling, and teaching!) and should effectively handle most difficult childhood behaviors. If you find yourself completely frustrated with your child's behavior and are relying on spanking as your primary discipline tool, please consult with a professional who can help you put some of these tools to work more effectively.

We have now covered the last part of our baseball diamond and our plan for addressing inappropriate childhood behavior is complete. Take time now to review the completed flowchart for responding to inappropriate behavior and finish the remaining section of your Parenting Plan.

## Steps for Responding to Your Child's Misbehavior

- Make sure that you are building a healthy relationship with your child.
- Consistently model appropriate parental behavior.
- Decide exactly what behavior you want your child to start doing.
- Make sure this behavior is specific and reasonable.
- Teach your child how to do the desired behavior, using either the Detour Method or Problem-Solving Steps.
- Consistently reward the desired behavior, using the Pour It On Technique and natural rewards.
- Make sure competing inappropriate behavior is not being accidentally rewarded.
- Design a simple contract if needed.
- Consistently use effective negative consequences when the inappropriate behavior occurs, choosing from Time-Out, natural consequences, logical consequences, ignoring, and response/cost.
- If you choose to use a mild spanking, do so only after the behavior strengthening and behavior weakening tools have been correctly and consistently used.

# It's All in Your Head

## Keeping Your Thoughts on Track

> Do not conform any longer to the pattern of this world, but be transformed by the renewing of your mind.
>
> Romans 12:2

Now that we have covered every base on our baseball diamond, I want to introduce you to an important principle that will help you use all of your tools as effectively as you possibly can. After all, what good is the best hammer in all the world if you are not able to hold onto it long enough to use it? How fast can a Ferrari go if you can't get your foot to the gas pedal?

Repeat the following sentence, increasing the intensity in your voice each time you say it: *I can't handle it! I can't handle it! I can't handle it!* Whatever your situation, chances are you won't be able to handle it if this is what you are

139

telling yourself. Our thoughts have a powerful effect on our ability to be godly and effective parents.

## What Are You Telling Yourself?

Have you ever thought about what you tell yourself when you are in a frustrating parenting situation? Sure, when everything is going fine and your children are acting like angels, it is easy to think positive thoughts. But what about when your darling five-year-old has just defiantly told you, "No!" after you so sweetly asked him to do something? Or when your ten-year-old screams at the top of her lungs that you don't love her anymore? Or what about when your three-year-old refuses to come out of the playroom at the local fast-food restaurant? Or when you have just had your fourth argument about homework in the last hour?

> Our thoughts have a powerful effect on our ability to be godly and effective parents.

What do you find yourself thinking when you are in the middle of one of these situations? Do any of these thoughts ring a bell?

If I have to tell him one more time . . .
This little monster is driving me up the wall!
I can't take it anymore!
What will the other parents think of me now?
How come only *my* kids act this way?
She's out to get me!

Where's the number for the adoption agency? I need it
now!

Sound familiar? If you are like the rest of us, statements
like these have gone through your mind a hundred times.
Maybe more. Telling yourself that your child must be related to Dr. Jekyll and Mr. Hyde, however, does not reduce
your frustration or help you respond to the situation more
effectively. Instead, it actually increases your frustration
and makes it more difficult for you to respond in a clear and
appropriate manner. Consider Jane, for example.

> Jane's children are having "one of those days" and it isn't
> even lunchtime yet. The toyroom is a mess, her oldest
> daughter is pestering her little brother, and her youngest
> child has not stopped whining since he woke up. Jane is
> on the verge of a meltdown and her frustration level is
> starting to peak.

What do you think will happen if Jane begins to fill her
mind with the kinds of thoughts we listed earlier? Will that
help her to keep a handle on her frustration or will it send
her frustration level into orbit? Will that make it easier for
her to stay in control of the situation or will she become
emotionally reactive to her child's behavior? Will that help
her respond to the problem behavior effectively or will it
cause her to respond ineffectively?

The fact is that the situation itself doesn't control Jane's
frustration level. Her thoughts do. If Jane's thoughts become negative, reactive, unrealistic, and pessimistic, then
her frustration level will quickly reach a boiling point. And
when Jane's thoughts send her into the danger zone, she
will find it much more difficult to respond to a challenging parenting situation in an effective way. Instead, she will
lose control and probably lose the battle.

## Renew Your Mind

Effective parenting does not happen without effective thinking. Make your thoughts both biblical and accurate: biblical because God's Word is truth and accurate (e.g., logically accurate) because it never helps to be telling yourself things that are simply not true. For example, consider this statement: *I'll never become a good parent.* This is the type of thought you might have after a particularly difficult day with your children. However, this thought is biblically inaccurate because it directly contradicts God's opinion about what and who you can become:

> Now to him who is able to do immeasurably more than all we ask or imagine, according to his power that is at work within us . . .
>
> Ephesians 3:20

and

> He who began a good work in you will carry it on to completion until the day of Christ Jesus.
>
> Philippians 1:6

*Effective parenting does not happen without effective thinking.*

It is also logically inaccurate because the fact that you have had a bad day or made a few parenting mistakes does not mean that you can't handle things differently tomorrow and get back on the road toward becoming the best parent you can be.

Or look at another common perception: *My son never listens to me.* While I have met many parents who have told this to themselves, I have seldom met a parent for whom this was entirely true. Most difficult children are not oppositional *all* the time. Mom and dad have become so tuned in to the negative behavior, however, that they either do not recognize the positive behavior or simply discount it when it happens. Therefore, they carry inaccurate thoughts about their child's behavior with them at all times. These thoughts have a negative effect on their frustration level, which has a negative effect on their parenting responses, which have a negative effect on their child's behavior, which has a negative effect on their thoughts, and so on. It quickly becomes a vicious cycle.

Look at what God has to say about the importance of biblical and accurate thinking:

> Do not conform any longer to the pattern of this world, but be transformed by the renewing of your mind. Then you will be able to test and approve what God's will is— his good, pleasing and perfect will. For by the grace given me I say to every one of you: Do not think of yourself more highly than you ought, but rather think of yourself with sober judgment, in accordance with the measure of faith God has given you.
>
> Romans 12:2–3

> . . . we take captive every thought to make it obedient to Christ.
>
> 2 Corinthians 10:5

> Finally, brothers, whatever is true, whatever is noble, whatever is right, whatever is pure, whatever is lovely, whatever is admirable—if anything is excellent or praiseworthy—think about such things.
>
> Philippians 4:8

Our thoughts are this important to God because they are the small but powerful rudder, hidden below the surface of the sea, that steers the ship. If your rudder is off course, your ship is headed for trouble. If your rudder is straight and true, you are on your way to reaching your destination.

## Setting Your Course

So how do you keep your thoughts both biblical and accurate? First you must avoid five common negative thinking traps[1] that plague many of us from time to time:

Overgeneralization—coming to a conclusion that is based on a single incident or piece of evidence and viewing an isolated negative event as a pattern that will continue forever. *I know we are going to have trouble with disrespect with this child.*

> Our thoughts are the small but powerful rudder that steers the ship.

Magnification—exaggerating the importance of mistakes and imperfections or making problems more significant than they really are. *It's terrible that my child still struggles with bedwetting.*

All-or-nothing thinking—seeing things in black-or-white categories and leaving no room for mistakes. If your performance falls short of perfection, you view yourself as a failure. *I am a lousy mother.*

Mind reading—assuming that you know what someone else is thinking or what his or her motivation for a certain behavior is and making quick judgments based on feelings or hunches. *He did that just to make me mad*. *Disqualifying the positive*—rejecting positive experiences by insisting that they "don't count" and focusing only on your child's negative behavior. *That girl never listens to me!*

Sound familiar? I thought so. Make a list of the negative thoughts you tend to think when confronted by a challenging or frustrating parenting situation.

**Situation**                                  **Negative Thought**

_____      _____

_____      _____

_____      _____

_____      _____

_____      _____

_____      _____

Now examine the biblical nature and accuracy of these thoughts by asking yourself the following questions:

1. Are these thoughts consistent with biblical teaching?
2. Do they represent God's point of view about my child, myself, or my family?
3. Are they consistent with the facts?
4. Are they overly negative or overly positive?
5. Is there any logical reasoning or evidence to support them?
6. Do they fall into a negative thinking trap?
7. Is there a better way to look at the situation?

Once you have examined your thoughts using these questions, the next step is to replace any unbiblical or inaccurate thoughts with thoughts that are both biblical and accurate. Following is a list of thoughts I have found helpful both in handling my own parenting frustrations and in my work with parents who needed a little rudder adjustment of their own.

"Calm down!" "Stay cool!" "Take it easy!" "Relax!"
"This is normal behavior for a child this age."
"Lord, please help me to handle this situation effectively."
"I want to make this a learning situation for my child."
"I must stay calm and *in control* if I want to be effective."
"Remember, my child is learning from how I act."
"What is the *most* effective thing I can do right now?"
"Maybe I need a few minutes to calm down and think."
"I need to stay focused on my parenting plan and use my tools."
"With God's help, I *can* handle this situation the way he desires."
"Lighten up; don't take things so seriously."
"Hundreds of other parents are going through this with their kids, just like I am."
"What others think doesn't matter. What matters is that I make this an effective learning situation for my child."
"I know this is hard, but I need to be consistent."
"My child is in the *process* of learning appropriate behaviors and mistakes are bound to happen."

These are the type of biblical and accurate thoughts that will help you handle difficult situations much more effectively! You need to choose several of these statements and customize them to work for you. Make up a few of your own statements that will help you keep your thoughts on track. Pick three or four and repeat them to yourself several times a day, write them down, say them in your sleep, memorize them! These thoughts need to become automatic so that they will be ready and waiting to help guide you in the right direction when a difficult parenting situation arises.

When strangling your child seems like the only thing you have not tried, replace unbiblical and inaccurate thoughts with more appropriate thoughts.

> "He's *trying* to make me mad" becomes "He's in the process of *learning* how to behave properly. How can I best teach him?"
>
> "She *never* listens, she doesn't care what I say!" becomes "Sometimes she doesn't listen, which makes me angry. But sometimes she does listen and I need to remember that."
>
> "He must have been switched at birth; he's a monster-child!" becomes "I need to be consistent and stick with my plan." (If you don't have a plan, see chapter 1!)
>
> "Everyone must think that I can't control my child!" becomes "What others think is not important now. What is important is that I be an effective parent."
>
> "She's been sent here to torture me!" becomes "With God's strength, I can handle this effectively."
>
> "I just can't take this anymore!" becomes "If I need help, I can easily consult with my doctor or a child therapist."

Remember Jane? What would happen if Jane were to re-place her old thoughts with thoughts that were biblical and accurate? She still might feel frustrated. However, she would have a much better chance of keeping her frustration level out of the danger zone and would probably respond in a more thoughtful and effective manner to the situation.

Take a few minutes to write down five thoughts that will be helpful for you. They may be thoughts from the list above or thoughts that you have come up with yourself.

_____

_____

_____

_____

_____

> While you can't control every choice your child makes, you can control the thoughts that go on inside your mind.

The good news is that while you can't control every choice your child makes, you can control the thoughts that go on inside your mind. If your thoughts are diving off the deep end, your feelings (and eventually your behavior) will throw on their bathing suits and jump right in after them. However, when you keep your thoughts biblical, accurate, and focused on the task at hand, they will help you respond more effectively to the problem situation.

Remember that your children can also fall into negative thinking traps. As you learn to keep your own thoughts biblical and accurate, you can also help your children learn to do the same. If you become aware that your child is viewing herself, another person, or a situation in an inaccurate manner, gently help her to look at the situation from other perspectives, or to consider the evidence for an alternative point of view. Ask guiding questions, such as:

"Have you thought of _____?"
"What do you think would happen if _____?"
"Does this ever happen to other kids?"
"What do you think God thinks about this?"
"What is the worst thing that could happen?"
"Do you think that there is any other way to explain it?"

These types of questions will help your child to think through the situation and learn to consider other, more accurate ways of viewing things. As children move through the elementary years, they will be increasingly able to benefit from this type of discussion. For younger children (e.g., four and five years old), you will need to keep the discussion very simple, focusing on only one or two ways of viewing a situation. This is a valuable skill that will help your child learn to view situations accurately and to handle the challenges that life will bring in a more effective manner.

Congratulations, you now have all the tools you need to hit a home run when responding to your child's challenging behavior. Just remember to tag each base of the baseball diamond and to keep your thoughts on track! Now let's take a look at how you can put your new skills to work.

# eight

# Let's Play Ball!

## Putting Your Plan to Work

All hard work brings a profit,
   but mere talk leads only to poverty.
                                    Proverbs 14:23

Your Parenting Plan should now be complete. We have covered each base of our baseball diamond and have talked about how you can put your thoughts to work for you as well. Now it's time to practice putting your plan into action. I have chosen seven common childhood problem situations that can prompt cardiac arrest for even the best of parents. I will go through these situations one by one, offering ideas and examples of how your new parenting tools can be effectively used in each situation. There are many different ways that you can address an area that needs attention. It will be up to you to choose the combination of ideas that seems most effective for your child. As you tackle a problem situation, review the chapter that discusses each base and remember to cover *all* of the bases. If your child does not seem to respond to your best attempts or if the

problem starts to get out of hand, please consult a qualified child therapist.

## Problem: Cleaning Up Toys

Situation: Jason's mother has to ask him at least three
or four times to get him to start picking up his toys. Jason
ignores his mother the first few times, then eventually starts
to comply, but only after she has yelled at him.

Keeping your thoughts on track: Think, "This is a common childhood problem," or "I need to handle this situation effectively."

### Pitcher's Mound: Building Strong Relationships

Make sure you are spending regular quality time with
Jason. Always communicate with respect and kindness. Be
willing to apologize to Jason (e.g., for yelling or poor anger-
control) when appropriate.

### First Base: Parental Modeling

Carefully model appropriate anger-control and respectful communication. Remember that Jason won't be moti-
vated to pick up his toys unless he sees you modeling neat-
ness and taking care of your own things.

### Second Base: Teaching Positive Behavior

Use the Detour Method to teach a replacement behavior:

- Decide: Steps may include Jason responding with,
  "Okay, Mom" and beginning to clean up at the first
  (or occasionally the second) request.
- Teach: Explain the steps to Jason and practice them
  together during positive times, remembering to provide specific verbal rewards as he learns his new
  steps.

- Review/rehearse: Occasionally quiz Jason on the steps and rehearse them a few times a week. The rehearsals should be brief, positive, and enjoyable.

### Third Base: Strengthening Positive Behavior

Use social rewards and the Pour It On Technique every time you see Jason use his steps (e.g., "Jason, you're picking up your toys the first time I asked you. Great job!"). Regularly point out the connection between the desired behavior and rewards (e.g., "Now that your toys are all picked up, we can get our pajamas on and read a story!"). Make sure inappropriate behavior is not rewarded by your attention or by you picking up the toys.

### Home Plate: Weakening Negative Behavior

Give clear, direct commands in a firm and respectful way (e.g., "Jason, I would like you to pick up your toys now."). If Jason respectfully offers a good reason to leave them out (e.g., he would like to play with them after dinner), allow this when appropriate. If Jason does not comply after the first request, ask once more, giving him the option of immediately putting his toys away or choosing a Time-Out. Following the Time-Out, have Jason immediately pick up the toys. If he refuses, have him return to Time-Out and administer the logical consequence of removing those toys for a specific period of time (one or two weeks) or removing a preferred activity (e.g., television) until the toys are picked up.

## Problem: Expressing Angry Feelings

Situation: When she is frustrated or things do not go her way, Kay tends to become very irritable and quick to shout and say hurtful things to other family members. Occasionally, she throws small objects (e.g., a pen) and stomps up to her room.

Keeping your thoughts on track: Think, "Kay will learn from how I respond," or "I need to calm down before I say anything."

### Pitcher's Mound: Building Strong Relationships

Build your relationship by showing interest in things that interest Kay. Always communicate to her with respect and kindness. Demonstrate that Kay is important to you by including her in your activities whenever possible.

### First Base: Parental Modeling

Model appropriate anger expression and respectful communication. Help Kay learn to handle her frustration by modeling patience and understanding when things don't go *your* way.

### Second Base: Teaching Positive Behavior

Make sure that your expectations for Kay are reasonable. Then, during a positive time, use Problem-Solving Steps with Kay to help her consider other ways to respond to frustrating situations. For example:

#### STOP AND STATE THE PROBLEM

After taking three deep breaths to cool down, Kay identifies the problem: "I feel angry when Mom won't let me take a phone call until my homework is finished."

#### THINK OF SOLUTIONS

Brainstorm with Kay to come up with possible solutions:

1. Scream and shout.
2. Throw something.

3. Get my homework finished so that I can use the phone.
4. Get more work done at school during study hall.
5. Go to my room to "cool down" instead of talking disrespectfully to my mom.
6. Tell my friends not to call until after 7:00 P.M.

### EVALUATE THE SOLUTIONS (KAY'S EVALUATIONS)

Allow Kay to evaluate each solution from her perspective. Then check to see if Kay's perspective matches your perspective:

Solution #1: Negative—will get me into trouble and make things worse.

Solution #2: Negative—will get me into trouble and make things worse.

Solution #3: Positive—will allow me to get on the phone more quickly.

Solution #4: Positive—will reduce the amount of homework I have to do.

Solution #5: Positive—will help me cool down and think instead of saying something in anger that I don't mean and that will hurt my mom.

Solution #6: Positive—will reduce the number of phone calls that come while I do my homework.

### PICK SOLUTIONS

Kay's evaluations leave four positive solutions (with which her parents agree). You and she agree to implement these.

1. Get more work done during study hall.
2. Tell my friends not to call until 7:00 P.M.
3. Get homework done more quickly at home.

4. Go to my room to "cool down" instead of talking disrespectfully when I can't use the phone because my homework is not finished.

### SEE IF IT WORKED

Kay will meet with you in one week to review her progress. You will also conduct brief rehearsals with Kay to get her used to using her plan and to review the likely consequences of her new approach.

## Third Base: Strengthening Positive Behavior

Consistently use social rewards and the Pour It On Technique when you see Kay using her plan and responding well when she cannot take a phone call (e.g., "Kay, I really appreciate the way you kept your cool just then when you couldn't talk to Susan on the phone. That was a great way to handle the situation."). Point out the natural reward of being able to use the phone when Kay's homework is completed and she has chosen to talk in a respectful way (e.g., "Well, Kay, your homework is done and you handled the situation when Susan called very well. So if you want to use the phone now, help yourself."). You may want to use a simple contract for a short time to help Kay improve her anger-control over a variety of situations. Consider using a response/cost approach if you do this. Finally, make sure that inappropriate anger expression *is not* rewarded with your immediate attention or by obtaining privileges or other rewards.

## Home Plate: Weakening Negative Behavior

Administer a Time-Out following any instance of clearly inappropriate anger expression (be specific!) or use the logical consequence of postponing any phone calls following homework completion by thirty minutes for each instance of inappropriate anger expression during homework time.

You can use a response/cost approach by using points and a menu or by dividing a preferred activity (e.g., talking on the phone, TV, video games) into time segments:

> To use points, help Kay create a menu of social and tangible rewards and give her a certain number of points (e.g., five) each day. She will lose one point for each inappropriate expression of anger. Remaining points may be used to purchase items from her menu.
>
> To use a preferred activity, such as talking on the phone, define phone call hours (e.g., from whenever homework is completed until 9:00 P.M.). Then divide Kay's phone call hours into thirty-minute segments. She will lose one segment for *each* inappropriate expression of anger.

If you have used Problem-Solving Steps with Kay, you may include her in a brainstorming discussion of various options for negative consequences when she displays her angry feelings in an inappropriate or disrespectful manner. Make it clear that you, the parents, will be choosing the negative consequences, but that you wanted to hear her ideas to help you decide which consequences would be the most helpful.

## Problem: Homework Completion

Situation: Tommy almost never gets his homework done on time. He usually starts a little before dinner, but is often found playing computer games in the den when his parents thought he was doing his homework in his room. As a result, homework takes all night, requires too many parental reminders, and sometimes does not get done by bedtime.

Keeping your thoughts on track: Try thinking, "This is very frustrating, but I will stick with my plan," or "I've got to be consistent even if I don't feel like it."

### Pitcher's Mound: Building Strong Relationships

When needed, provide reasonable help with Tommy's school projects and homework. Address misbehavior in a firm but loving manner. Through it all, focus on enjoying your relationship with Tommy.

### First Base: Parental Modeling

Model timely completion of your household duties and maintain a reasonable "work-before-play" approach regarding your own tasks. Don't forget to model respectful communication.

### Second Base: Teaching Positive Behavior

Use Problem-Solving Steps together with Tommy to consider various ways of handling this situation. For example:

#### STOP AND STATE THE PROBLEM

Tommy: "You guys always bug me about doing my homework and I wish you would just let me take care of it myself."

Parents: "We are concerned because your homework frequently does not get finished and we have to constantly remind you to get back to work. This is very frustrating for us because it happens every night and is a frequent source of conflict."

#### THINK OF SOLUTIONS

A brainstorming session will produce solutions such as the following:

1. Let Tommy get his homework done entirely on his own.
2. No free time activities until all Tommy's homework is completed and checked by parents.

3. Have some type of reward if Tommy's homework gets completed and checked by a designated time for five consecutive nights and then for ten consecutive nights.

4. Let Tommy do his homework on his own with no parental reminders. If his homework is not completed and checked by bedtime on two occasions during any two-week period, then implement the second option for one month.

5. Use a homework log that is initialed for accuracy by Tommy's teacher.

6. If Tommy engages in a free time activity prior to homework completion, he will lose that activity for the rest of the evening.

7. Assess parents a "nagging fine" of $1.00 for each time they nag.

#### EVALUATE THE SOLUTIONS

Each person should give a "+" or a "–" rating for each solution. They may look something like this:

| Solution | Tommy | Mom | Dad |
|---|---|---|---|
| #1 Tommy do on own | + | – | – |
| #2 No free time activity until done | – | + | + |
| #3 Reward for five and ten days | + | + | + |
| #4 Tommy do on own, no reminders | + | + | + |
| #5 Homework log | – | + | + |
| #6 Lose free time activity | – | + | + |
| #7 Nagging fine for parents | + | + | + |

#### PICK SOLUTIONS

Choose several solutions upon which everyone agrees:

1. Use a signed homework log so that parents have an accurate record of Tommy's homework assignments.

2. Let Tommy do homework on his own with the expectation that his parents will check it each night against his homework log. Parents will be assessed a $1.00 "nagging fine" for any reminders about homework prior to the final nightly check. If Tommy's homework is not completed and checked before bedtime on any two occasions during any two-week period, Tommy will move to the following step.

3. With the exception of a brief after-school break (e.g., twenty minutes), Tommy will begin homework after school and will need to have his homework completed and checked by parents prior to *any* free time activities. If Tommy engages in a free time activity prior to his homework being completed, he will lose that privilege for the rest of the day.

4. Tommy will receive a predetermined reward (e.g., rent a video of choice, have a friend over) for five consecutive days of homework completion by 7:30 P.M. without any arguing. A different reward can then be earned for ten consecutive days.

### See If It Worked

Review Tommy's progress on homework completion together in one week. Then fine-tune the plan as needed.

### Third Base: Strengthening Positive Behavior

Consistently use the Pour It On Technique and social rewards when Tommy shows the desired homework behavior (e.g., "Tommy, you're really working hard on your homework. You'll have it done before you know it. Good job!"). Point out the natural rewards of positive homework behavior (e.g., "Now that your homework is done, you can play video games for a little while before bed. Way to get it done."). You might want to try a simple contract linking consecutive nights of timely homework completion without arguing to a predetermined reward, as was decided upon in the problem-solving discussion.

### Home Plate: Weakening Negative Behavior

As determined in the problem-solving discussion, Tommy's failure to responsibly complete his homework on his own will result in his having to adhere to a more structured after-school schedule. In the more structured plan, Tommy's choice to prolong the time it takes to complete his homework will result in less free time afterward. Any free time activity Tommy engages in *prior* to homework completion and parents checking his work will result in the loss of that activity for the day. As another logical consequence, any homework assignments that Tommy has failed to complete during the week must be finished before he can participate in any weekend free time activities.

## Problem: Interrupting

Situation: Julie has developed a bad habit of interrupting her parents, particularly when they are talking on the telephone.

Keeping your thoughts on track: Consider, "This happens to lots of other parents too," or "I need to help Julie learn that interrupting does not get my attention."

### Pitcher's Mound: Building Strong Relationships

Take time to answer Julie's questions whenever possible. On a regular basis let her know that you love her. Include Julie in your activities as often as you can.

### First Base: Parental Modeling

Model respectful communication, waiting until others are finished talking before you speak. Also model patience when you have to wait for things (e.g., stoplights, slow drivers, long checkout lines).

### Second Base: Teaching Positive Behavior

Use the Detour Method to teach Julie a replacement behavior:

- Decide: Steps may include the following. Julie will wait quietly until mom or dad finishes talking. If it is important, she will say, "Excuse me," in a nice voice. Then, she will wait quietly for a response.
- Teach: Teach Julie these steps, taking turns modeling them for her and having her do them. Be sure to let her know in which situations it is appropriate to interrupt you (e.g., emergencies). Pretend you are talking on the telephone as you practice and provide lots of social rewards as Julie learns her new replacement behavior.
- Review/rehearse: Several times a week, rehearse the steps with Julie. You can even have a friend call you just so you can practice. Quiz Julie on her new steps, giving her plenty of social rewards and even a small tangible reward as she memorizes them. Make it fun!

### Third Base: Strengthening Positive Behavior

When the telephone rings, remind Julie to use her steps and anticipate that she will do a great job (e.g., "Julie, the telephone is ringing. Use your steps now while I'm on the telephone."). Use the Pour It On Technique and social rewards when Julie uses her steps in both rehearsals and real situations (e.g., "Julie, you did a great job saying, 'Excuse me,' and waiting while I was on the phone. That was wonderful!"). Give her social rewards *immediately* following the positive behavior. You may even want to excuse yourself from your conversation for a moment to answer her question and give her a specific verbal reward *during* your conversation. Also connect natural rewards with Julie's positive behavior by surprising her with a special treat or fun activity following positive telephone behavior (e.g., "Since you did such a great job waiting while I was on the telephone, why don't we sit down and read one of our favorite books right now!").

### Home Plate: Weakening Negative Behavior

Remind Julie of the negative consequences that will follow repeated interrupting (e.g., Time-Out) *before* getting on the telephone. If she interrupts your call, remind her to use her steps, walk away, and provide as little attention as possible. If she continues to follow you around or interrupts twice during any conversation, send Julie to Time-Out.

## Problem: Not Following Directions

Situation: While Danny listens to his parents some of the time, they often have to repeat a command three or four times before he actually starts to respond.

Keeping your thoughts on track: Tell yourself, "I need to stay focused on my parenting plan and use my tools," or pray, "Lord, help me handle this situation effectively."

### Pitcher's Mound: Building Strong Relationships

Spend positive "one-on-one" time with Danny, clearly communicating that you enjoy being with him. Then address his misbehavior in a firm but loving manner.

### First Base: Parental Modeling

Model respectful communication by listening and responding when someone talks to you or asks you a question. When someone asks you for help, always try to respond with a willing attitude. Consistently model good anger-control skills for Danny to imitate.

### Second Base: Teaching Positive Behavior

Use the Detour Method to teach Danny a replacement behavior:

- Decide: Use the "Just Do It" steps. Danny's first step is to just do it (e.g., Say, "Okay, Mom."). If he has a question or a comment, he will ask or speak in a respectful way. If the answer to his question is no, then he will just do it. If necessary, he can talk to you about it later.
- Teach: Explain these steps to Danny and practice them together, role-playing situations in which Danny has been noncompliant in the past. Make the instruction brief and enjoyable, providing plenty of positive feedback as he learns his new steps. Print them on the computer along with a graphic of his choice.
- Review/rehearse: Quiz Danny on his steps, giving him a nickel each time he can repeat them five times in a row. Rehearse the steps together several times a week, using common noncompliance situations for role-plays and helping him to learn how to handle these situations differently.

### Third Base: Strengthening Positive Behavior

Use social rewards and the Pour It On Technique to help you become more aware of instances when Danny is compliant and to make sure that they are rewarded (e.g., "Danny, you just listened the first time I asked you to get your coat. That was great!"). Point out the connection between compliance and natural rewards (e.g., "Since you've been listening so well this afternoon, you can watch TV."). Make sure noncompliant behavior is not being rewarded by your attention or by Danny being able to effectively avoid or postpone the requested task. You may also use a simple contract to improve compliance by rewarding every day of good listening behavior with a point or token. If Danny saves up ten points, he can earn a special activity with his dad (e.g., working on the car, going fishing, etc.).

### Home Plate: Weakening Negative Behavior

Make your requests of Danny in a firm but respectful way. If he does not comply following your first request, offer him a clear choice between listening and choosing a Time-Out or logical consequence. If he does not comply within five to eight seconds, administer the Time-Out or inform him of the logical consequence in a matter-of-fact manner.

Use logical consequences whenever possible. For instance, if Danny is refusing to turn off the television, offer him a choice between immediately listening and losing the privilege of watching television for the rest of the day. Following a negative consequence, always remind Danny that he can make a better choice next time.

If Danny's noncompliance continues to be a problem, create a system in which increased instances of blatant noncompliance (e.g., not listening following two or more clear parental requests) result in an increased loss of privileges. For example, while each instance of noncompliance may result in a Time-Out, four instances in one day may *also* earn the loss of television and computer games for the day. Five instances may result in the additional loss of playing with certain toys for the day and six may result in going to bed early. Discuss the possible negative consequences with Danny ahead of time and record the number of Time-Outs on a chart as a visual reminder.

## Problem: Sibling Squabbles

Situation: Sarah and Teresa are constantly bickering and fighting when using each other's belongings.

Keeping your thoughts on track: Try thinking, "I've got to make sure the right behaviors are rewarded," or, "I must stay calm and in control if I want to be effective."

### Pitcher's Mound: Building Strong Relationships

Play together and build memories with your family. Spend time teaching your children about God. Emphasize love and respect for others, clear and honest communication, and forgiveness.

### First Base: Parental Modeling

Model positive problem-solving skills that utilize respectful communication when you have a problem to solve. Be willing to forgive and to look at a situation from another's point of view.

### Second Base: Teaching Positive Behavior

Engage both girls together in the Problem-Solving Steps. The results might look something like this:

#### STOP AND STATE THE PROBLEM

Each girl should count to five before talking or arguing when upset with the other. Then each should state the problem from her viewpoint:

Sarah: "She is always barging into my room and taking my things without asking. That really makes me mad."

Teresa: "I do use some of Sarah's things without asking, but she uses mine too, and I don't mind. I'm frustrated that she is making such a big thing of this."

### Think of Solutions

Have the girls work together to compile a list of possible solutions:

1. Neither uses the other's belongings.
2. Personal belongings may only be used with permission.
3. Certain specified items may be used without permission while other items may be used only with permission.
4. Neither can go into the other's room without permission.
5. If a person violates the agreed-upon rules, there will be a negative consequence for that person.
6. If the amount of sibling squabbling decreases substantially for a certain length of time, both girls will receive a special privilege.
7. If both girls engage in arguing or fighting, there will be immediate negative consequences for both, regardless of who started the argument.
8. If one girl violates the agreed-upon rules, the other should try to handle it informally and appropriately by talking with her sister. If the sister who has violated the rules does not cooperate, the other girl should then discuss the situation with her parents.

### Evaluate the Solutions

Both girls and both parents should rate each solution:

| Solution | Sarah | Teresa | Mom | Dad |
|---|---|---|---|---|
| #1 Do not use each other's things | – | – | – | – |
| #2 Can use with permission | – | – | – | – |
| #3 Use only some things | + | + | + | + |
| #4 Permission to enter other's room | + | – | – | – |
| #5 Violator receives negative consequence | + | + | + | + |
| #6 Reward if squabbling decreases | + | + | + | + |

| #7 Negative consequence for squabble | – | – | + | + |
| #8 When one breaks a rule | + | + | + | + |

### Pick Solutions

Based on the evaluations, make a list of acceptable solutions:

1. Make a list of personal items that may be used only with permission (e.g., clothes).
2. Make a list of personal items that, if not in use, may be used without asking permission (e.g., games, CDs).
3. For all other personal items, ask permission if the owner is present, otherwise use with care.
4. If one sister violates the rules, the other sister should try to resolve it informally. If this does not work or if the violations continue, talk with parents. The "violating" sister will receive a negative consequence to be determined by parents.
5. If *both* girls become verbally inappropriate (e.g., shouting, name-calling), both will receive an immediate Time-Out, regardless of who started the argument. If they do this twice in one day, both will go to bed thirty minutes early that evening.
6. If one girl damages the other's property, she will be required to immediately replace it from her allowance.
7. If the girls reduce their squabbles to only two during a one-week period, they can both go to a movie that weekend. If they reduce squabbles to only two during a two-week period, they can each have a friend sleep overnight.

### See If It Worked

Meet together as a family in one week to review progress. Update permission lists and fine-tune the plan as needed.

### Third Base: Strengthening Positive Behavior

Consistently use the Pour It On Technique with both girls individually and as a pair (e.g., "Teresa, you just did a great job responding to Sarah. I'm proud of you because I know that was difficult" or "You girls have both done a wonderful job today of working things out and getting along. Way to go!"). Emphasize the natural rewards of getting along (e.g., "Since you girls have been getting along so well lately, why don't we all go out to a movie tonight?"). Make sure arguing and fighting are not rewarded with your attention and use a simple contract to reward positive sibling behavior as was decided in the problem-solving discussion.

### Home Plate: Weakening Negative Behavior

As decided upon in the problem-solving discussion, administer a Time-Out to both girls following instances of mutual arguing or fighting. Follow two or more instances in a day with a logical consequence (e.g., to bed thirty minutes earlier) for each girl *in addition to* the Time-Out. As decided upon in the problem-solving discussion, administer a logical consequence (e.g., loss of television, free time, or phone privileges for the day) to any girl who violates the agreed-upon rules. The nonviolating sister will not receive a negative consequence if she handles herself appropriately.

If you desire, a response/cost approach can be used where the girls as a team would be given three points each day. They would lose one point for each instance of sibling squabbling in which both girls clearly behave inappropriately. Points remaining at the end of the day are awarded to both girls (e.g., if there are two points left, each girl gets two points) and they may purchase items from their individual menus with these points. The key is that points are kept or lost as a team.

## Problem: Temper Tantrums

Situation: Trevor is a young boy who throws temper tantrums several times a week and sometimes several times a day.

Keeping your thoughts on track: Tell yourself, "With God's help, I can handle this situation," or, "What others think doesn't matter. What matters is that I make this an effective learning situation for Trevor."

### Pitcher's Mound: Building Strong Relationships

Address misbehavior in a firm but loving manner. Spend one-on-one time with Trevor and regularly remind him that you love him.

### First Base: Parental Modeling

Model respectful communication and appropriate expression of angry feelings. Maintain a flexible and patient attitude when things do not go your way.

### Second Base: Teaching Positive Behavior

Use the Detour Method to teach Trevor an alternative behavior:

- Decide: Try steps like the following. Trevor will count to three or five before saying, "I feel _____ (mad, sad, frustrated, disappointed, etc.)" in a respectful way. Then he will either do what he has been asked or find something else to do, when appropriate.
- Teach: Practice these steps with Trevor, role-playing situations that commonly result in tantrums. Model the steps and then allow Trevor to practice them. Help him count to three, identify what he might be feeling (e.g., mad, sad), and follow through with what you

have asked or find something else to do (depending on the situation).

- Review/rehearse: Review these steps with Trevor several times each week. Use tantrum situations from the prior week for your role-plays and remember to keep them fun and rewarding. Help Trevor identify the positive consequences of using his steps (e.g., will have more fun, won't go to Time-Out) as well as the negative consequences of a tantrum (e.g., goes to Time-Out). Teach Trevor that it is okay for him to feel sad or mad, but that he needs to express his feelings with respectful words. Quiz Trevor on his steps to help him learn them, print them out on the computer, or have him draw a picture of himself using the steps.

### Third Base: Strengthening Positive Behavior

Use the Pour It On Technique to provide Trevor with social rewards during rehearsals and in real life when you see him using his steps. Remind him to use the steps to help prevent a tantrum when you see one on the horizon. Watch for Trevor to stop his tantrum more quickly and begin to use his steps. When he does this, *immediately* follow this with positive attention (e.g., "Trevor, you did a great job just now of calming down and saying your feelings in a nice voice. That's how to do it!"). Point out the natural rewards that follow more appropriate anger-control (e.g., "Trevor, since you have done such a nice job staying calm today, especially when I asked you to come inside this afternoon, how would you like to play one of your favorite games?").

Do not reward tantrums by following them with your attention or by giving in to your child's demands. You can use a simple contract for tantrums by providing Trevor with a token or sticker for each time period (e.g., morning, afternoon, evening) in which no tantrums are thrown. These tokens can then be used to purchase items from his menu.

A response/cost approach can also be used, as described below.

### Home Plate: Weakening Negative Behavior

When possible, ignore Trevor's tantrums by looking away or walking away, letting Trevor know that he can get your attention *only* by calming down (e.g., "Trevor, if you want to talk to me, you need to calm down and use your words."). Give him as little attention as possible until he begins to calm down.

If Trevor follows you around the house with a "walking" tantrum or if you are not in a situation where ignoring is permissible, offer him one final choice between using his steps and choosing a Time-Out. If he does not begin to calm down within five to eight seconds, immediately administer the Time-Out in a matter-of-fact manner. For some children, being sent to their room to cool off until they are able to come out and talk in a calm and respectful way is an effective logical consequence. For others, a Time-Out will be needed.

Provide logical consequences for multiple tantrums throughout the day. For example, even if each tantrum results in a Time-Out, three tantrums in one day could also result in the loss of a favorite privilege for the day (e.g., television and computer games). Four tantrums would result in the loss of this privilege and going to bed thirty minutes earlier.

A response/cost approach can be used for tantrums by giving a certain number of tokens or stickers each day and having Trevor lose one token for each tantrum. The tokens left at the end of the day are his to keep and may be used to purchase social or tangible rewards from his menu. An alternative option is to divide a preferred activity (e.g., playing Nintendo) into time segments (e.g., two fifteen-minute segments). Each segment is represented by a coupon and one coupon is lost for each tantrum.

Your goal is to be the best parent you can be. To accomplish this you need a plan. Now you have one. Begin with the opening pitch of relationship building, then continue around the bases of modeling, teaching, rewarding, and disciplining. Through it all, remember to stay on course by keeping your thoughts biblical and accurate. As the challenges of parenting come your way, stick to your plan! Don't forget that even the great Babe Ruth struck out many times. He was called the "home run king," though, because he always kept swinging and never gave up. God has great plans for you and your family. Be a vital part of his plan by becoming the best parent you can be!

# *Appendix A*

# Your Parenting Plan

Here is your Parenting Plan. You can use this plan to take inventory on your overall progress as a parent or to help you put together a plan of action for addressing a particular problem behavior. This form can be photocopied for your personal use.

After filling in your name, complete section A by writing down the goal for which you are using the Parenting Plan. Your goal will be either to evaluate your overall parenting progress or to help your child improve a certain behavior. Next, complete section B by rating yourself in each of the five key areas: building healthy relationships, modeling biblical and appropriate behavior, teaching your children appropriate behavior, effectively strengthening positive behavior, and effectively weakening negative behavior. This rating will give you an idea of which areas need improvement. For each area that needs improvement, begin by reviewing the chapter that corresponds with that area. Then, complete section C by writing down specific ways you can improve your parenting approach in each area. For example, you may decide to improve your relationship with your child by scheduling family time together and by finding ways to remind him that you love him. You might decide to use Problem-Solving Steps with your child to teach her how to respond to difficult situations more effectively. Once you have decided upon the improvements that you would like to make, be sure to share them with your spouse or a close friend who will help you be accountable to making these important changes. Finally, put your plan to work and hit a home run!

# Parenting Plan

Parent Name: _____

A. Goal: _____

_____

B. Areas to evaluate (check all that apply):

| Area | Strong | Needs Improvement |
|---|---|---|
| 1. Building healthy relationships (e.g., quality, quantity, communication) | ☐ | ☐ |
| 2. Modeling biblical and appropriate behavior (e.g., marital relationship, anger-control, priorities, etc.) | ☐ | ☐ |
| 3. Teaching children appropriate behaviors | ☐ | ☐ |
| 4. Effectively strengthening appropriate behaviors | ☐ | ☐ |
| 5. Effectively weakening inappropriate behaviors | ☐ | ☐ |

C. Ways to improve in each area:

| Area | | Ways to Improve |
|---|---|---|
| 1. Building healthy relationships | a. | _____ |
| | b. | _____ |
| 2. Modeling biblical and appropriate behavior | a. | _____ |
| | b. | _____ |
| 3. Teaching children appropriate behaviors | a. | _____ |
| | b. | _____ |
| 4. Effectively strengthening appropriate behaviors | a. | _____ |
| | b. | _____ |
| 5. Effectively weakening inappropriate behaviors | a. | _____ |
| | b. | _____ |

# Appendix B

# Tools for the Journey

The following worksheets are provided to help you get the most out of the parenting tools we have discussed. You may photocopy them for your personal use. The first worksheet is to be used to rate your relationship with your child and then to have your spouse or a close friend rate this relationship. If you want honest feedback, this is a good way to get it. The second worksheet will help you identify areas to improve in your relationship with your child, "first steps" that you need to take to make those improvements, and someone who will help keep you accountable for making these important changes.

The Modeling Worksheet gives you a chance to list characteristics that you would like to see in your child and then to rate the quality of that characteristic in your own life. You can also write down a problem behavior that your child is displaying (e.g., shouting when mad) and rate your behavior in that area. Finally, you have an opportunity to list specific changes that you would like to make in your own behavior that will help you model and teach appropriate behavior to your children.

There are two worksheets for the Detour Method. On the first worksheet, write down your child's problem behavior and then develop a list of replacement steps for your child to take *instead* of repeating the problem behavior, as discussed in chapter 4. Once you have arrived at a set of replacement steps that are simple and within your child's ability level, use the second worksheet to record those steps and teach them to your child. For the occasions when you use Problem-Solving Steps with your child or together as a family, I have provided an evaluation sheet that you can use to list possible solutions and everyone's ratings.

The last three worksheets are designed to help you with your behavior strengthening tools. When starting to use the Pour It On Technique, use this next worksheet to help you keep track of how often you are giving social rewards to your child. This is a great way to train yourself to make social rewards a regular part of your parenting vocabulary. When a simple contract is in order, use the blank contract provided to write down a description of the desired behaviors, their respective point values, and the appropriate signatures. I have also included a Menu you can use to list the social and/or tangible rewards that your child can earn with his or her points. Finally, for older children, I have included a Daily Behavior Chart that may be used to keep track of behaviors and the amount of points that your child has earned and spent.

# Rate Your
# Parent/Child Relationship

Parent name: _____

Child name: _____

## Self Rating

| 1 | 2 | 3 | 4 | 5 |
|---|---|---|---|---|
| terrible | needs work | fair | good | excellent |


Parent name: _____

Child name: _____

## Spouse's/Friend's Rating

| 1 | 2 | 3 | 4 | 5 |
|---|---|---|---|---|
| terrible | needs work | fair | good | excellent |

# Relationship Building Plan

*What are three things that I can improve in my relationship with my child?*

1. _____

   _____

   _____

2. _____

   _____

   _____

3. _____

   _____

   _____

*What is the first step I must take to make each of these improvements a reality?*

1. _____

   _____

   _____

2. _____

   _____

   _____

3. _____

   _____

   _____

*Whom will I ask to keep me accountable for making these changes?*

Name: _____

# Modeling Worksheet

| Desired Characteristics | Rating in Parent's Life | | |
|---|---|---|---|
| | good | fair | poor |
| _____ | ☐ | ☐ | ☐ |
| _____ | ☐ | ☐ | ☐ |
| _____ | ☐ | ☐ | ☐ |
| _____ | ☐ | ☐ | ☐ |
| _____ | ☐ | ☐ | ☐ |
| _____ | ☐ | ☐ | ☐ |
| _____ | ☐ | ☐ | ☐ |
| _____ | ☐ | ☐ | ☐ |

| Problem Behavior | My Behavior | | |
|---|---|---|---|
| | good | fair | poor |
| _____ | ☐ | ☐ | ☐ |
| _____ | ☐ | ☐ | ☐ |
| _____ | ☐ | ☐ | ☐ |
| _____ | ☐ | ☐ | ☐ |
| _____ | ☐ | ☐ | ☐ |

**Changes I Will Make to Model Positive Behavior**

_____    _____
_____    _____
_____    _____
_____    _____
_____    _____
_____    _____
_____

# Detour Method Worksheet

**Problem Behavior**          **Replacement Behavior**

1._____    a. _____

                                    b. _____

                                    c. _____

                                    d. _____

                                    e. _____

                                    f. _____

**Problem Behavior**          **Replacement Behavior**

2._____    a. _____

                                    b. _____

                                    c. _____

                                    d. _____

                                    e. _____

                                    f. _____

# Detour Method Steps

Behavior: _____

STEPS:

1. _____
   _____
   _____
   _____

2. _____
   _____
   _____

3. _____
   _____
   _____

4. _____
   _____
   _____

5. _____
   _____
   _____

6. _____
   _____
   _____

# Problem-Solving Evaluation Sheet

| Possible Solutions | Names and Ratings (+/−) | | | |
|---|---|---|---|---|
|  |  |  |  |  |
|  |  |  |  |  |
|  |  |  |  |  |
|  |  |  |  |  |
|  |  |  |  |  |
|  |  |  |  |  |
|  |  |  |  |  |
|  |  |  |  |  |
|  |  |  |  |  |
|  |  |  |  |  |
|  |  |  |  |  |
|  |  |  |  |  |
|  |  |  |  |  |
|  |  |  |  |  |
|  |  |  |  |  |
|  |  |  |  |  |
|  |  |  |  |  |

# Pour It On Technique

Complete the following chart for any two days within a one-week period. Place an "x" in one box for every time you give your child a social reward for an appropriate behavior on that day. Repeat this exercise as often as needed until giving social rewards becomes a natural part of your life.

**Day:** _____ **Target behavior(s):**_____

☐☐☐☐☐☐☐☐☐☐☐☐☐☐☐☐☐☐☐☐☐☐☐☐☐☐☐☐

**Day:** _____ **Target behavior(s):**_____

☐☐☐☐☐☐☐☐☐☐☐☐☐☐☐☐☐☐☐☐☐☐☐☐☐☐☐☐

# Contract

This is a contract between _____ and
_____. _____ agrees to
do the behaviors listed in the manner agreed upon and described below. In return,
_____ agree(s) to provide points as described below, which can
be used to purchase items from the menu. All points will be awarded on the same day that
they are earned and menu items will be provided within a reasonable time frame.

**Behaviors**      **Point Value**

1. _____ _____
Description:


2. _____ _____
Description:


3. _____ _____
Description:


4. _____ _____
Description:



I have read this contract and agree to the behaviors and point values listed above.

Date: _____
Signed: _____      Signed: _____

# Menu

| Item | Price |
| --- | --- |

# Daily Behavior Chart

Name: _____

| Behavior | Point Value | Mon | Tues | Wed | Thurs | Fri | Sat | Sun |
|---|---|---|---|---|---|---|---|---|
| | | | | | | | | |
| | | | | | | | | |
| | | | | | | | | |
| | | | | | | | | |
| | | | | | | | | |
| | | | | | | | | |
| | | | | | | | | |
| | | | | | | | | |
| | | | | | | | | |
| | | | | | | | | |
| | | | | | | | | |
| | | | | | | | | |
| Points Earned Today | | | | | | | | |
| Points Spent Today | | | | | | | | |
| Total Points Remaining | | | | | | | | |

# *Appendix* C

# Your Child's Development

The developmental work of Jean Piaget and Erik Erikson provides us with foundational knowledge of child development. This knowledge will help you understand how children develop their thinking abilities and the nature of the social challenges that tend to accompany different ages. This, in turn, will facilitate a better understanding of your child's behavior and will help you develop reasonable expectations and appropriate responses that help your child successfully move through each important stage of development. The suggested ages below are approximate. Some children reach these stages on a slightly faster or slower timetable.

## Birth to Eighteen Months

### *Thinking Abilities*

Your child learns about the world through the senses and through repeated experience. Gradually, your child will develop object permanence, the ability to view objects as being separate from himself or herself.

### Social Challenges

Erikson labeled this stage as basic trust versus mistrust. The goal is for your child to develop a sense of trust and to learn that the world is a safe place. This sense of trust forms the basis for later stages of development.

### Things to Do

Provide a stimulating environment with lots of brightly colored objects, room for exploration, and plenty of interaction. Promptly meet your child's physical and emotional needs, create a safe environment, and maintain appropriate behavioral limits.

## Eighteen Months to Three

### Thinking Abilities

Children increase their ability to use language to communicate. However, they still see the world only from their own viewpoint and are not able to logically reason or thoughtfully consider the consequences of their actions.

### Social Challenges

With increasing abilities, toddlers are learning to do many things on their own that previously had to be done for them. They have an increased awareness of themselves as individuals and understandably want more independence. However, they cannot do all that they would like due to physical limitations, safety concerns, and time constraints. Their verbal skills and patience are still developing, and all of this is new to them, which explains their need for reassurance, tendency to cling, and penchant for throwing tantrums.

### Things to Do

This stage serves as a building block for the development of self-esteem and self-confidence. Whenever possible, let your child do as much as he or she is able to do, offer a pre-determined set of choices, and provide gentle assistance. Both excessive parental control and a lack of opportunity for autonomy delay skill-building and your child's development of confidence in his or her abilities.

## Three to Five

### Thinking Abilities

Still seeing the world very much from their own viewpoint and not yet being able to reason logically, these preschool-age children also experience what is known as "magical thinking." They believe that what they think is real. You guessed it. Santa Claus, the tooth fairy, and monsters are real to them. Not surprisingly, fears and nightmares appear frequently during this stage.

### Social Challenges

At this age, children tend to show increased initiative, become self-motivated and active, and enjoy learning new things. They can now cooperatively interact with other children in creative play. The goal is to help your child develop the skills to succeed in and enjoy these new peer relationships and to develop a positive attitude toward learning and exploration.

### Things to Do

As these children are not yet logical thinkers, reasoning often doesn't relieve their common fears (e.g., monsters under the bed). Concrete responses such as night-lights, examining the room together, and reassurance that you will protect them are often useful. Help them develop "mastery" over the feared object through play. Create an environment that encourages and rewards learning and trying new things. Help your child to learn basic social behaviors (e.g., taking turns, sharing) that will aid his or her interactions with peers. Criticism or overcontrol may inhibit self-confidence and contribute to the fear that he or she is doing something wrong or cannot succeed without parental direction.

## Six to Twelve

### Thinking Abilities

Children now begin to understand the reasons for rules and can link consequences with behavior. They can take in different aspects of a situation and understand that there can be more than one possible solution to a problem. Their ability to understand a situation from another person's point of view also begins to develop at this time. The ability to think abstractly and engage in complex reasoning, however, is still out of reach.

### Social Challenges

The child has now entered the world of school and peers and must master academic tasks and learn important social skills for success both now and in later years. The goal is to help these children succeed in both of these areas as their ability to have successful academic and social experiences and to respond effectively to negative experiences will have a significant impact on their developing self-view.

### Things to Do

Without taking over, do what you can to help your child succeed in the areas of school and peer relationships by helping him or her develop good study habits and by maintaining open communication with teachers, fostering realistically positive expectations, being consistent with reasonable behavioral limits, and obtaining additional help if needed (e.g., tutoring, therapy). As always, keep your relationship with your child strong by spending one-on-one time together as well as time together as a family. Teach your children to effectively handle failures and disappointments and to develop a balanced view of themselves. Guide them in learning positive ways to relate with peers and effective methods for solving peer and family problems. Encourage them to consider other people's feelings and require them to treat others with respect. Make sure that your child knows how positively God thinks of him or her. Provide lots of positive feedback and encouragement, gradually helping your child to develop the self-confidence and skills that will help him or her successfully manage the teenage years that are just around the corner.

# Notes

### Chapter 1: *You Need a Plan*

1. Stephen R. Covey, *The Seven Habits of Highly Effective People* (New York: Simon & Schuster, 1989).

### Chapter 4: *Let's Do This Instead*

1. This problem-solving process was developed by T. J. D'Zurilla and M. R. Gold-fried, "Problem Solving and Behavior Modification," *Journal of Abnormal Psychology* 78 (1971), 107–26.

### Chapter 5: *Make Them Glad They Did It*

1. Several of the ideas presented here on the effective use of social rewards and simple contracts are adapted from the research and clinical work of the following psychologists: R. Barkley, *Defiant Children: A Clinician's Manual for Parent Training* (New York: Guilford Press, 1987); R. Forehand and R. McMahon, *Helping the Noncompliant Child: A Clinician's Guide to Parent Training* (New York: Guilford Press, 1981); G. Patterson, *Families* (Champaign, Ill.: Research Press, 1975); and C. Webster-Stratton and M. Herbert, *Troubled Families—Problem Children* (New York: Wiley, 1994).

2. Forehand and McMahon (1981) refer to these three types of social rewards as labeled verbal rewards, unlabeled verbal rewards, and physical rewards.

### Chapter 6: *This Has Gotta Stop!*

1. Several of the ideas presented here on the use of Time-Out and the response/cost approach are adapted from the research and clinical work of several psychologists. See chapter 5, note 1 for more information.

2. My thanks to Jeffrey Prater, Ph.D. for allowing me to use several of his helpful ideas on the effective use of Time-Out, as presented in "Clinical Child Psychology" at the Graduate School of Psychology, Fuller Theological Seminary, 1991.

3. For an excellent discussion of biblical interpretation, see Gordon Fee and Douglas Stewart, *How to Read the Bible for All It's Worth* (Grand Rapids: Zondervan, 1982).

### Chapter 7: *It's All in Your Head*

1. Commonly referred to as cognitive distortions, this list of negative thinking traps is based on the work by the following authors: A. T. Beck, A. J. Rush, B. F. Shaw, and G. Emery, *Cognitive Therapy of Depression* (New York: Guilford Press, 1979) and D. D. Burns, *Feeling Good: The New Mood Therapy* (New York: William Morrow, 1980).

Todd Cartmell, Psy.D., is a licensed clinical psychologist who holds a doctorate in clinical psychology from Fuller Theological Seminary. He is currently part of a group private practice in Wheaton, Illinois, where he specializes in work with children and adolescents. Dr. Cartmell speaks regularly on parenting and children's issues to church, parachuch, and community groups. He and his wife have two young children.